TO

FROM

DATE

REAL LIFE

DEVOTIONS

AND

FUNNY STORIES

FOR WOMEN

REAL LIFE

DEVOTIONS

AND

FUNNY STORIES

FOR WOMEN

Introduction

I t's undeniable—this old world has more than enough troubles to go around. What we need are more Christian women who are really willing to honor God with their prayers and their service. Hopefully, you are determined to be such a woman—a woman who walks in wisdom as she offers counsel and direction to her family, to her friends, and to her coworkers.

In your hands, you hold a book that contains 100 devotional readings for Christian women like you. These pages contain wisdom from God's Word, ideas for managing your life, insights from noted Christian thinkers, plus a little dash of humor tossed in for good measure.

During the next 100 days, try this experiment: read a chapter each day. If you're already committed to a daily time of worship, this book will enrich that experience. If you are not, the simple act of giving God a few minutes each morning will change the direction and the quality of your life.

Every day provides opportunities to love, to laugh, and to put God where He belongs: at the center of your life. It's up to you to seize these opportunities, and the sooner you begin, the better. So why not begin today?

Who's First?

Do not worship any other gods besides me.

Exodus 20:3 NLT

Who is in charge of your heart? Is it God, or is it someone or something else? Have you given Christ your heart, your soul, your talents, your time, and your testimony? Or are you giving Him little more than a few hours each Sunday morning?

In the book of Exodus, God warns that we should place no gods before Him. Yet all too often, we place our Lord in second, third, or fourth place as we worship other things. When we unwittingly place possessions or relationships above our love for the Creator, we create big problems for ourselves.

Does God rule your heart? Make certain that the honest answer to this question is a resounding yes. In the life of every radical believer, God comes first. And that's precisely the place that He deserves in your heart.

When all else is gone, God is still left. Nothing changes Him.

Hannah Whitall Smith

To God be the glory, great things He has done; so loved He the world that He gave us His Son.

Fanny Crosby

Our ultimate aim in life is not to be healthy, wealthy, prosperous, or problem free. Our ultimate aim in life is to bring glory to God.

Anne Graham Lotz

COMING SOON TO A CHURCH SIGN NEAR YOU ...

GIVE GOD WHAT'S RIGHT—
NOT WHAT'S LEFT!

GOD DOESN'T WANT SHARES OF YOUR LIFE;
HE WANTS CONTROLLING INTEREST!

IF GOD IS YOUR CO-PILOT ...
SWAP SEATS!

Very Big Plans

Teach me to do Your will, for You are my God.
May Your gracious Spirit lead me on level ground.

Psalm 143:10 HCSB

The Bible makes it clear: God's got a plan—a very big plan—and you're an important part of that plan. But here's the catch: God won't force His plans upon you; you've got to figure things out for yourself . . . or not.

As a follower of Christ, you should ask yourself this question: "How closely can I make my plans match God's plans?" The more closely you manage to follow the path that God intends for your life, the better.

Do you have questions or concerns about the future? Take them to God in prayer. Do you have hopes and expectations? Talk to God about your dreams. Are you carefully planning for the days and weeks ahead? Consult God as you establish your priorities. Turn every concern over to your Heavenly Father, and sincerely seek His guidance—prayerfully, earnestly, and often. Then, listen for His answers . . . and trust the answers that He gives.

REAL INSIGHTS

The God who created and numbers the stars in the heavens also numbers the hairs of my head. He pays attention to very big things and to very small ones. What matters to me matters to Him, and that changes my life.

Elisabeth Elliot

We will stand amazed to see the topside of the tapestry and how God beautifully embroidered each circumstance into a pattern for our good and His glory.

Joni Eareckson Tada

God prepared a plan for your life alone—and neither man nor the devil can destroy that plan.

Kay Arthur

A pastor was shaking hands after the big Easter sermon when a seldom-seen parishioner passed by. The pastor grabbed the man's hand and pulled him aside. The pastor said, "Friend, you need to join the Army of the Lord!" The man sheepishly replied, "I'm already in the Army of the Lord, Pastor." The pastor then asked, "So how come I only see you at Christmas and Easter?" The man whispered back, "I'm in the secret service."

Love According to God

Now these three remain: faith, hope, and love.
But the greatest of these is love.

1 Corinthians 13:13 HCSB

Love, like everything else in this wonderful world, begins and ends with God, but the middle part belongs to us. During the brief time that we have here on earth, God has given each of us the opportunity to become a loving person—or not. God has given each of us the opportunity to be kind, to be courteous, to be cooperative, and to be forgiving—or not. God has given each of us the chance to obey the Golden Rule, or to make up our own rules as we go. If we obey God's rules, we're safe, but if we do otherwise, we're headed for trouble in a hurry.

The Christian path is an exercise in love and forgiveness. If you are to walk in Christ's footsteps, you must forgive those who have done you harm, and you must accept Christ's love by sharing it freely with family, friends, neighbors, and even strangers.

God does not intend for you to experience mediocre relationships; He created you for far greater things. Building lasting relationships requires compassion, wisdom, empathy, kindness, courtesy, and forgiveness. If that sounds a lot like work, it is—which is perfectly fine with God.

Why? Because He knows that you are capable of doing that work, and because He knows that the fruits of your labors will enrich the lives of your loved ones and the lives of generations yet unborn.

REAL INSIGHTS

It is when we come to the Lord in our nothingness, our powerlessness and our helplessness that He then enables us to love in a way which, without Him, would be absolutely impossible.

Elisabeth Elliot

Those who abandon ship the first time it enters a storm miss the calm beyond. And the rougher the storms weathered together, the deeper and stronger real love grows.

Ruth Bell Graham

COMING SOON TO A CHURCH SIGN NEAR YOU...

IF YOU'RE A CHRISTIAN,
EARTH IS THE ONLY HELL
YOU'LL EVER KNOW!
IF YOU'RE NOT A CHRISTIAN,
EARTH IS THE ONLY HEAVEN
YOU'LL EVER KNOW.

CARS AREN'T THE ONLY THING
RECALLED BY THEIR MAKER.

The Book God Wrote

For I am not ashamed of the gospel, because it is God's power for salvation to everyone who believes.

Romans 1:16 HCSB

Do you read your Bible a lot . . . or not? The answer to this simple question will determine, to a surprising extent, the quality of your life and the direction of your faith.

As you establish priorities for life, you must decide whether God's Word will be a bright spotlight that guides your path every day or a tiny nightlight that occasionally flickers in the dark. The decision to study the Bible—or not—is yours and yours alone. But make no mistake: how you choose to use your Bible will have a profound impact on you and your loved ones.

The Bible is unlike any other book. It is a priceless gift from your Creator, a tool that God intends for you to use in every aspect of your life. And, it contains promises upon which you, as a Christian, can and must depend. God's Holy Word is a priceless, one-of-a-kind treasure. Handle it with care, but more importantly, handle it every day.

REAL INSIGHTS

Study the Bible and observe how the persons behaved and how God dealt with them. There is explicit teaching on every condition of life.

Corrie ten Boom

The Bible is a remarkable commentary on perspective. Through its divine message, we are brought face to face with issues and tests in daily living and how, by the power of the Holy Spirit, we are enabled to respond positively to them.

Luci Swindoll

The Reference Point for the Christian is the Bible. All values, judgments, and attitudes must be gauged in relationship to this Reference Point.

Ruth Bell Graham

COMING SOON TO A CHURCH SIGN NEAR YOU ...

PSALMS READ HERE.

READ THE BIBLE.
IT'S USER-FRIENDLY
PLUS WE OFFER TECH SUPPORT
HERE ON SUNDAYS AT 10 A.M.

A Rule That's Golden

Just as you want others to do for you, do the same for them.

Luke 6:31 HCSB

Would you like to make the world a better place? If so, you can start by being a girlfriend who practices the Golden Rule.

Some rules are easier to understand than they are to live by, and the Golden Rule certainly fits that description. Jesus told us that we should treat other people in the same way that we would want to be treated. But sometimes, especially when we're tired, upset, jealous, or insecure, that rule is very hard to follow.

Jesus wants us to treat other people with respect, kindness, courtesy, and love. When we do, we make our families and friends happy . . . and we make our Father in heaven very proud.

So if you're wondering how to make the world a better place, here's a great place to start: let the Golden Rule be your rule, too. And if you want to know how to treat other people, ask the woman you see every time you look into the mirror. The answer you receive from her will tell you exactly what to do.

REAL INSIGHTS

The Golden Rule starts at home, but it should never stop there.

Marie T. Freeman

It is one of the most beautiful compensations of life that no one can sincerely try to help another without helping herself.

Barbara Johnson

I have discovered that when I please Christ, I end up inadvertently serving others far more effectively.

Beth Moore

COMING SOON TO A CHURCH SIGN NEAR YOU...

THE TASK AHEAD OF US IS NEVER
AS GREAT AS THE POWER BEHIND US.

GOD GRADES ON THE CROSS,
NOT THE CURVE.

COME WORK FOR THE LORD.
THE WORK IS HARD, THE HOURS ARE LONG,
AND THE PAY IS LOW, BUT THE RETIREMENT
BENEFITS ARE OUT OF THIS WORLD.

Behaving Differently

So don't get tired of doing what is good.
Don't get discouraged and give up,
for we will reap a harvest of blessing at the appropriate time.

Galatians 6:9 NLT

Okay, answer this question honestly: Do you behave differently because of your relationship with Jesus? Or do you behave in pretty much the same way that you would if you weren't a believer? Hopefully, the fact that you've invited Christ to reign over your heart means that you've made BIG changes in your thoughts and your actions.

Doing the right thing is not always easy, especially when you're tired or frustrated. But, doing the wrong thing almost always leads to trouble. And sometimes, it leads to big trouble.

If you're determined to follow "the crowd," you may soon find yourself headed in the wrong direction. So here's some advice: Don't follow the crowd—follow Jesus. And keep following Him every day of your life.

Either God's Word keeps you from sin, or sin keeps you from God's Word.

Corrie ten Boom

REAL INSIGHTS

There may be no trumpet sound or loud applause when we make a right decision, just a calm sense of resolution and peace.

Gloria Gaither

Although God causes all things to work together for good for His children, He still holds us accountable for our behavior.

Kay Arthur

COMING SOON TO A CHURCH SIGN NEAR YOU . . .

WHEN YOUR GOOD BEHAVIOR
SPEAKS FOR ITSELF . . .
DON'T INTERRUPT.

IF YOU CAN'T BE AN
"ONWARD CHRISTIAN SOLDIER,"
AT LEAST DON'T PASS THE AMMUNITION
TO THE ENEMY.

YOU CAN'T COMPROMISE
AND CONQUER SIN AT THE SAME TIME.

What Kind of Example?

You should be an example to the believers in speech,
in conduct, in love, in faith, in purity.

1 Timothy 4:12 HCSB

Whether we like it or not, all of us are role models. Our friends and family members watch our actions and, as followers of Christ, we are obliged to act accordingly.

What kind of example are you? Are you the kind of woman whose life serves as a genuine example of righteousness? Are you a woman whose behavior serves as a positive role model for young people? Are you the kind of woman whose actions, day in and day out, are based upon kindness, faithfulness, and a love for the Lord? If so, you are not only blessed by God, but you are also a powerful force for good in a world that desperately needs positive influences such as yours.

Corrie ten Boom advised, "Don't worry about what you do not understand. Worry about what you do understand in the Bible but do not live by." And that's sound advice because our families and friends are watching . . . and so, for that matter, is God.

Living life with a consistent spiritual walk deeply influences those we love most.

Vonette Bright

A stressed out woman was tailgating the car in front of her. As the car in front slowed quickly for a red light, the tailgater became frustrated and laid on the horn. But she didn't stop there. The frustrated tailgater shook her fist at the driver ahead as he waited for the light to change. But before he had time to move his car, the angry woman was accosted by a police officer who tapped on the driver-side window. The policeman instructed the woman to get out of her car and put her hands up.

The angry woman was hauled off to the local police station where she was fingerprinted, photographed, and placed in a holding cell. But after a couple of hours, the policeman opened the cell door and released the angry woman.

As they were walking out of the station, the policeman offered an apology: "I'm sorry for this mistake. You see, I pulled up behind your car while you were blowing your horn and cussing up a blue streak. Meanwhile, I noticed your 'What Would Jesus Do?' bumper sticker, the 'Follow Me to Sunday School' widow decal, and your chrome-plated Christian fish emblem on the trunk. Naturally, I assumed the car was stolen."

Listening to God

The one who is from God listens to God's words. This is why
you don't listen, because you are not from God.

John 8:47 HCSB

Sometimes God speaks loudly and clearly. More often, He speaks in a quiet voice—and if you are wise, you will be listening carefully when He does. To do so, you must carve out quiet moments each day to study His Word and sense His direction.

Can you quiet yourself long enough to listen to your conscience? Are you attuned to the subtle guidance of your intuition? Are you willing to pray sincerely and then to wait quietly for God's response? Hopefully so. Usually God refrains from sending His messages on stone tablets or city billboards. More often, He communicates in subtler ways. If you sincerely desire to hear His voice, you must listen carefully, and you must do so in the silent corners of your quiet, willing heart.

When we come to Jesus stripped of pretensions, with a needy spirit, ready to listen, He meets us at the point of need.

Catherine Marshall

We cannot experience the fullness of Christ if we do all the expressing. We must allow God to express His love, will, and truth to us.

Gary Smalley

God is always listening.

Stormie Omartian

SMILE!

An old gentleman was walking through the park one day when he came upon a little boy sitting on a bench. The boy was busily saying his ABCs. The old man waited until the child was finished and then said, "I see you're practicing your alphabet."

"No," replied the boy. "I was praying. You see, I don't know how to pray very well, so I just give God the letters, and He makes them into the right words!"

Do You Believe in Miracles?

With God's power working in us, God can do much, much more than anything we can ask or imagine.

Ephesians 3:20 NCV

D o you believe that God is at work in the world? And do you also believe that nothing is impossible for Him? If so, then you also believe that God is perfectly capable of doing things that you, as a mere human being with limited vision and limited understanding, would deem to be utterly impossible. And that's precisely what God does.

Since the moment that He created our universe out of nothingness, God has made a habit of doing miraculous things. And He still works miracles today. Expect Him to work miracles in your own life, and then be watchful. With God, absolutely nothing is impossible, including an amazing assortment of miracles that He stands ready, willing, and able to perform for you and yours.

REAL INSIGHTS

I could go through this day oblivious to the miracles all around me or I could tune in and "enjoy."

Gloria Gaither

Faith means believing in realities that go beyond sense and sight. It is the awareness of unseen divine realities all around you.

Joni Eareckson Tada

God specializes in things thought impossible.

Catherine Marshall

Larry, out of the blue, decided to go ice fishing. He had never been before, so he borrowed an auger and some tackle and headed out alone.

He walked out on the ice and starting auguring the hole when he heard a voice from above say, "There are no fish under the ice." Larry looked around, and seeing no one, continued to auger.

Once again, a deep, resounding voice from above said, "There are no fish under the ice."

Larry looked up and asked, "Is that you, God?" The voice replied, "NO, this is the arena manager."

When People Are Cruel

Kind people do themselves a favor,
but cruel people bring trouble on themselves.

Proverbs 11:17 NCV

Face it: sometimes people can be cruel . . . very cruel. When other people are unkind to you or to your friends, you may be tempted to strike back, either verbally or in some other way. Don't do it! Instead, remember that God corrects other people's behaviors in His own way, and He doesn't need your help (even if you're totally convinced that He does!). Remember that God has commanded you to forgive others, just as you, too, must sometimes seek forgiveness from others.

So, when other people behave cruelly, foolishly, or impulsively—as they will from time to time—don't be hotheaded. Instead, speak up for yourself as politely as you can, and walk away. Then, forgive everybody as quickly as you can, and leave the rest up to God.

A keen sense of humor helps us to overlook the unbecoming, understand the unconventional, tolerate the unpleasant, overcome the unexpected, and outlast the unbearable.

Billy Graham

You can be sure you are abiding in Christ if you are able to have a Christlike love toward the people that irritate you the most.

Vonette Bright

There were two evil brothers. They were both rich, and they used their money to keep their evil ways hidden from the public eye. They even attended the same church and appeared to be perfect Christians.

One day, their pastor retired, and a new one was hired. Not only could the new pastor see right through the brothers' deception, but he also spoke well and true, and the church membership grew in numbers. So in time, the new pastor kicked off a fund-raising campaign to build a new sanctuary.

Suddenly one night, one of the evil brothers died. Before the funeral, the surviving brother sought out the new pastor and handed him a check for the amount needed to finish paying for the new building.

"I have only one condition," said the brother. "At the funeral, you must say my brother was a saint." The pastor gave his word, and deposited the check.

The next day, at the funeral, the pastor did not hold back. "He was an evil man," he said. "He cheated on his wife and abused his family." After going on like this for about fifteen minutes, the pastor finally concluded, "But, compared to his brother, he was a SAINT."

Beyond Fear

Even when I walk through the dark valley of death,
I will not be afraid, for you are close beside me.
Your rod and your staff protect and comfort me.

Psalm 23:4 NLT

We live in a world that is, at times, a frightening place. We live in a world that is, at times, a discouraging place. We live in a world where life-changing losses can be so painful and so profound that it seems we will never recover. But, with God's help, and with the help of encouraging family members and friends, we can recover.

During the darker days of life, we are wise to remember the words of Jesus, who reassured His disciples, saying, "Take courage! It is I. Don't be afraid" (Matthew 14:27 NIV). Then, with God's comfort and His love in our hearts, we can offer encouragement to others. And by helping them face their fears, we can, in turn, tackle our own problems with courage, determination, and faith.

REAL INSIGHTS

Fear and doubt are conquered by a faith that rejoices. And faith can rejoice because the promises of God are as certain as God Himself.

Kay Arthur

When once we are assured that God is good, then there can be nothing left to fear.

Hannah Whitall Smith

Worry is a cycle of inefficient thoughts whirling around a center of fear.

Corrie ten Boom

THE GEEK'S PRAYER

The Lord is my programmer, I shall not crash. He installed His software on the hard disk of my heart. All of His commands are user-friendly. His directory guides me to the right choices for His name's sake. Even though I scroll through the problems of life, I will fear no bugs, for He is my back-up. His password protects me. He prepares a menu before me in the presence of my enemies. His help is only a keystroke away. Surely goodness and mercy will follow me all the days of my life and my file will be merged with His and saved forever. Amen

God's Gifts to You

Each one has his own gift from God,
one in this manner and another in that.

1 Corinthians 7:7 NKJV

God has given you an array of talents, and He has given you unique opportunities to share those talents with the world. Your Creator intends for you to use your talents for the glory of His kingdom in the service of His children. Will you honor Him by sharing His gifts? And, will you share His gifts humbly and lovingly? Hopefully you will.

The old saying is both familiar and true: "What you are is God's gift to you; what you become is your gift to God." As a woman who has been touched by the transforming love of Jesus Christ, your obligation is clear: You must strive to make the most of your own God-given talents, and you must encourage your family and friends to do likewise.

Today, make this promise to yourself and to God: Promise to use your talents to minister to your family, to your friends, and to the world. And remember: The best way to say "Thank You" for God's gifts is to use them.

REAL INSIGHTS

The Lord has abundantly blessed me all of my life. I'm not trying to pay Him back for all of His wonderful gifts; I just realize that He gave them to me to give away.

Lisa Whelchel

God has given you special talents—now it's your turn to give them back to God.

Marie T. Freeman

Not everyone possesses boundless energy or a conspicuous talent. We are not equally blessed with great intellect or physical beauty or emotional strength. But we have all been given the same ability to be faithful.

Gigi Graham Tchividjian

A kindergarten teacher gave her class a "show and tell" assignment. The students were instructed to bring objects that represented their religions.

The first student stood before the class and said, "My name is Benjamin, I am Jewish, and this is a Star of David."

The second student stood up and said, "My name is Mary. I'm a Catholic, and this is a Rosary."

The third student got up and said, "My name is Tommy. I am Baptist, and this is a casserole."

Optimistic Christianity

*My cup runs over. Surely goodness and mercy
shall follow me all the days of my life;
and I will dwell in the house of the Lord Forever.*

Psalm 23:5-6 NKJV

Face facts: pessimism and Christianity don't mix. Why? Because Christians have every reason to be optimistic about life here on earth and life eternal. Mrs. Charles E. Cowman advised, "Never yield to gloomy anticipation. Place your hope and confidence in God. He has no record of failure."

Sometimes, despite our trust in God, we may fall into the spiritual traps of worry, frustration, anxiety, or sheer exhaustion, and our hearts become heavy. What's needed is plenty of rest, a large dose of perspective, and God's healing touch, but not necessarily in that order.

Today, make this promise to yourself and keep it: vow to be a hope-filled Christian. Think optimistically about your life, your education, your family, and your future. Trust your hopes, not your fears. Take time to celebrate God's glorious creation. And then, when you've filled your heart with hope, share your optimism with others. They'll be better for it, and so will you. But not necessarily in that order.

REAL INSIGHTS

If you can't tell whether your glass is half-empty or half-full, you don't need another glass; what you need is better eyesight . . . and a more thankful heart.

Marie T. Freeman

Make the least of all that goes and the most of all that comes. Don't regret what is past. Cherish what you have. Look forward to all that is to come. And most important of all, rely moment by moment on Jesus Christ.

Gigi Graham Tchividjian

Q & A

Q. Where is the first tennis match mentioned in the Bible?
A. When Joseph served in Pharaoh's court.

Q. Who was the greatest financier in the Bible?
A. Noah. He was floating his stock while everyone else was in liquidation.

Q. What do Winnie the Pooh and John the Baptist have in common?
A. Same middle name.

Making Peace with the Past

Do not remember the past events, pay no attention to things of old. Look, I am about to do something new; even now it is coming. Do you not see it? Indeed, I will make a way in the wilderness, rivers in the desert.

Isaiah 43:18-19 HCSB

Have you made peace with your past? If so, congratulations. But, if you are mired in the quicksand of regret, it's time to plan your escape. How can you do so? By accepting what has been and by trusting God for what will be.

Because you are human, you may be slow to forget yesterday's disappointments; if so you are not alone. But if you sincerely seek to focus your hopes and energies on the future, then you must find ways to accept the past, no matter how difficult it may be to do so.

If you have not yet made peace with the past, today is the day to declare an end to all hostilities. When you do, you can then turn your thoughts to the wondrous promises of God and to the glorious future that He has in store for you.

REAL INSIGHTS

Whoever you are, whatever your condition or circumstance, whatever your past or problem, Jesus can restore you to wholeness.

Anne Graham Lotz

Yesterday is just experience but tomorrow is glistening with purpose—and today is the channel leading from one to the other.

Barbara Johnson

Shake the dust from your past, and move forward in His promises.

Kay Arthur

COMING SOON TO A CHURCH SIGN NEAR YOU ...

EVERY SAINT HAS A PAST—
EVERY SINNER HAS A FUTURE!

EVERY TIME THE DEVIL
REMINDS YOU OF YOUR PAST ...
REMIND HIM OF HIS FUTURE—AND YOURS!

TODAY IS A GIFT FROM GOD.
THAT'S WHY IT IS CALLED "THE PRESENT."

Your Bright Future

"I say this because I know what I am planning for you,"
says the Lord. "I have good plans for you, not plans
to hurt you. I will give you hope and a good future."

Jeremiah 29:11 NCV

L et's talk for a minute about the future . . . your future. How bright do you believe your future to be? Well, if you're a faithful believer, God has plans for you that are so bright that you'd better pack several pairs of sunglasses and a lifetime supply of sunblock!

The way that you think about your future will play a powerful role in determining how things turn out (it's called the "self-fulfilling prophecy," and it applies to everybody, including you). So here's another question: Are you expecting a terrific tomorrow, or are you dreading a terrible one? The answer to that question will have a powerful impact on the way tomorrow unfolds.

Today, as you live in the present and look to the future, remember that God has an amazing plan for you. Act—and believe—accordingly. And one more thing: don't forget the sunblock.

REAL INSIGHTS

The future lies all before us. Shall it only be a slight advance upon what we usually do? Ought it not to be a bound, a leap forward to altitudes of endeavor and success undreamed of before?

Annie Armstrong

Do not limit the limitless God! With Him, face the future unafraid because you are never alone.

Mrs. Charles E. Cowman

A pastor of a large church and a taxi driver both died and went to heaven. St. Peter was at the pearly gates waiting for them. "Come with me," said St. Peter to the taxi driver. The taxi driver did exactly as he was told and followed St. Peter to a mansion. It had anything you could imagine, from a bowling alley to an Olympic-size pool. "Wow, thank you," said the taxi driver.

Next, St. Peter led the pastor to a rugged old shack with a bunk bed and a little black-and-white television set. "Wait, I think you are a little mixed up," said the pastor. "Shouldn't I be the one who gets the mansion? After all I was an important pastor; I had many responsibilities; and I preached the gospel."

"Yes, that's true," said St. Peter. "But during your sermons everybody slept. And when the taxi driver drove, everyone prayed."

Sharing His Peace

*And the peace of God, which surpasses all comprehension,
will guard your hearts and your minds in Christ Jesus.*

Philippians 4:7 NASB

The beautiful words of John 14:27 give us hope: "Peace I leave with you, my peace I give unto you." Jesus offers us peace, not as the world gives, but as He alone gives. We, as believers, can accept His peace or ignore it.

When we accept the peace of Jesus Christ into our hearts, our lives are transformed. And then, because we possess the gift of peace, we can share that gift with fellow Christians, family members, friends, and associates. If, on the other hand, we choose to ignore the gift of peace—for whatever reason—we cannot share what we do not possess.

As every woman knows, peace can be a scarce commodity in a demanding, 21st-century world. How, then, can we find the peace that we so desperately desire? By turning our days and our lives over to God. Elisabeth Elliot writes, "If my life is surrendered to God, all is well. Let me not grab it back, as though it were in peril in His hand but would be safer in mine!" May we give our lives, our hopes, and our prayers to the Lord, and, by doing so, accept His will and His peace.

REAL INSIGHTS

God's peace is like a river, not a pond. In other words, a sense of health and well-being, both of which are expressions of the Hebrew shalom, can permeate our homes even when we're in white-water rapids.

Beth Moore

Let's please God by actively seeking, through prayer, "peaceful and quiet lives" for ourselves, our spouses, our children and grandchildren, our friends, and our nation (1 Timothy 2:1-3 NIV).

Shirley Dobson

The fruit of our placing all things in God's hands is the presence of His abiding peace in our hearts.

Hannah Whitall Smith

COMING SOON TO A CHURCH SIGN NEAR YOU ...

NO JESUS, NO PEACE;
KNOW JESUS, KNOW PEACE!

A PEACEFUL HEART FINDS JOY
IN ALL OF LIFE'S SIMPLE PLEASURES.

SOME HEARTS NEED A PACE-MAKER;
ALL HEARTS NEED THE PEACE-MAKER.

Choices

*But Daniel purposed in his heart
that he would not defile himself . . . .*

Daniel 1:8 KJV

Face facts: your life is a series of choices. From the instant you wake up in the morning until the moment you nod off to sleep at night, you make countless decisions—decisions about the things you do, decisions about the words you speak, and decisions about the way that you choose to direct your thoughts.

As a believer who has been transformed by the radical love of Jesus, you have every reason to make wise choices. But sometimes, when the daily grind threatens to grind you up and spit you out, you may make choices that are displeasing to God. When you do, you'll pay a price because you'll forfeit the happiness and the peace that might otherwise have been yours.

So, as you pause to consider the kind of Christian you are—and the kind of Christian you want to become—ask yourself whether you're sitting on the fence or standing in the light. And then, if you sincerely want to follow in the footsteps of the One from Galilee, make choices that are pleasing to Him. He deserves no less . . . and neither, for that matter, do you.

REAL INSIGHTS

God is voting for us all the time. The devil is voting against us all the time. The way we vote carries the election.

Corrie ten Boom

Commitment to His lordship on Easter, at revivals, or even every Sunday is not enough. We must choose this day—and every day—whom we will serve. This deliberate act of the will is the inevitable choice between habitual fellowship and habitual failure.

Beth Moore

Faith is not a feeling; it is action. It is a willed choice.

Elisabeth Elliot

SMILE!

One beautiful Sunday morning, the pastor announced to his congregation: "My good people, I have here in my hands three sermons—a $100 sermon that lasts five minutes, a $50 sermon that lasts fifteen minutes, and a $10 sermon that lasts a full hour. Now, we'll take the collection and see which one you've chosen."

He's Here

Draw near to God, and He will draw near to you.

James 4:8 HCSB

Do you ever wonder if God really hears your prayers? If so, you're in good company: lots of very faithful Christians have wondered the same thing. In fact, some of the biggest heroes in the Bible had their doubts—and so, perhaps, will you. But when you have your doubts, remember this: God isn't on vacation, and He hasn't moved out of town. God isn't taking a coffee break, and He isn't snoozing on the couch. He's right here, right now, listening to your thoughts and prayers, watching over your every move.

As the demands of everyday life weigh down upon you, you may be tempted to ignore God's presence or—worse yet—to rebel against His commandments. But, when you quiet yourself and acknowledge His presence, God touches your heart and restores your spirits. So why not let Him do it right now?

If your heart has grown cold, it is because you have moved away from the fire of His presence.

Beth Moore

REAL INSIGHTS

If you want to hear God's voice clearly and you are uncertain, then remain in His presence until He changes that uncertainty. Often, much can happen during this waiting for the Lord. Sometimes, he changes pride into humility, doubt into faith and peace.

Corrie ten Boom

Our souls were made to live in an upper atmosphere, and we stifle and choke if we live on any lower level. Our eyes were made to look off from these heavenly heights, and our vision is distorted by any lower gazing.

Hannah Whitall Smith

Children lined up in the cafeteria of a Christian school for lunch. At the head of the table was a large pile of apples.

Next to the apples, someone had written a note that read, "Take only one, God is watching."

At the other end of the table was a large pile of chocolate chip cookies.

One little boy wrote his own note and snuck it next to the cookies, "Take all you want, God is watching the apples."

Whose Expectations?

My dear friends, don't let public opinion influence how you live out our glorious, Christ-originated faith.

James 2:1 MSG

Expectations, expectations, expectations! As a woman in the 21st century, you know that demands can be high, and expectations even higher. The media delivers an endless stream of messages that tell you how to look, how to behave, how to eat, and how to dress. The media's expectations are impossible to meet—God's are not. God doesn't expect you to be perfect . . . and neither should you.

Remember: the expectations that really matter are God's expectations. Everything else takes a back seat. So do your best to please God, and don't worry too much about what other people think. And, when it comes to meeting the unrealistic expectations of a world gone nuts, forget about trying to be perfect—it's impossible.

If you try to be everything to everybody, you will end up being nothing to anybody.

Vance Havner

TOP TEN REASONS GOD CREATED EVE

10. God was worried that Adam would frequently become lost in the garden because he would not ask for directions.

9. God knew that one day Adam would require someone to locate and hand him the remote.

8. God knew Adam would never go out and buy himself a new fig leaf when his wore out and would therefore need Eve to buy one for him.

7. God knew Adam would never be able to make a doctor's, dentist, or haircut appointment for himself.

6. God knew Adam would never remember which night to put the garbage on the curb.

5. God knew if the world was to be populated, men would never be able to handle the pain and discomfort of childbearing.

4. As the Keeper of the Garden, Adam would never remember where he left his tools.

3. Apparently, Adam needed someone to blame his troubles on when God caught him hiding in the garden.

2. As the Bible says, it is not good for man to be alone!

1. When God finished the creation of Adam, He stepped back, scratched his head, and said, "I can do better than that!"

Questions, Questions, Questions

Now if any of you lacks wisdom, he should ask God, who gives to all generously and without criticizing, and it will be given to him. But let him ask in faith without doubting. For the doubter is like the surging sea, driven and tossed by the wind.

James 1:5-6 HCSB

God doesn't explain Himself to us with the clarity that we humans would prefer (think about this: if God did explain Himself with perfect clarity, we wouldn't have enough brainpower to understand the explanation that He gave).

When innocent people are hurt, we question God because we can't figure out exactly what He's doing, or why. Why are innocent people allowed to feel pain and good people allowed to die? Since we can't fully answer those kinds of questions now, we must trust in God's love, God's wisdom, and God's plan.

And while we're waiting for that wonderful day (in heaven) when all our questions will be answered, we should use the time that we have here on earth to help the people who need it most. After all, we'll have plenty of time to have our questions answered when we get to heaven. But when it comes to helping our neighbors, we don't have nearly that much time. So let's get busy helping . . . right now!

REAL INSIGHTS

When there is perplexity there is always guidance—not always at the moment we ask, but in good time, which is God's time. There is no need to fret and stew.

Elisabeth Elliot

We are finding we don't have such a gnawing need to know the answers when we know the Answer.

Gloria Gaither

Q & A

Q. How did Adam and Eve feel when expelled from the Garden of Eden?
A. They were really put out.

Q. What is one of the first things that Adam and Eve did after they were kicked out of the garden?
A. They really raised Cain.

Q. What excuse did Adam give to his children as to why he no longer lived in Eden?
A. Your mother ate us out of house and home.

His Commandments

Teach me Your way, O LORD; I will walk in Your truth.

Psalm 86:11 NASB

God gave us His commandments for a reason: so that we might obey them and be blessed. Oswald Chambers, the author of the Christian classic devotional text, *My Utmost for His Highest*, advised, "Never support an experience which does not have God as its source, and faith in God as its result." These words serve as a powerful reminder that, as Christians, we are called to walk with God and obey His commandments. But, we live in a world that presents us with countless temptations to stray far from God's path. We Christians, when confronted with sin, have clear instructions: Walk—or better yet run—in the opposite direction.

The Holy Bible contains thorough instructions which, if followed, lead to fulfillment, righteousness, and salvation. But, if we choose to ignore God's commandments, the results are as predictable as they are tragic.

A righteous life has many components: faith, honesty, generosity, love, kindness, humility, gratitude, and worship, to name but a few. If we seek to follow the steps of our Savior, Jesus Christ, we must seek to live according to His commandments. Let us follow God's commandments, and let us conduct our lives in such a way that we might be shining examples for those who have not yet found Christ.

REAL INSIGHTS

Don't worry about what you do not understand. Worry about what you do understand in the Bible but do not live by.

Corrie ten Boom

Only grief and disappointment can result from continued violation of the divine principles that underlie the spiritual life.

A. W. Tozer

The Ten Commandments were given to evoke fear and reverence for the Holy One so that obedience and blessing might result.

Beth Moore

SMILE!

A Sunday school teacher was discussing the Ten Commandments with her five- and six-year-olds.

After explaining the commandment to "honor thy father and thy mother," she asked, "Is there a commandment that teaches us how to treat our brothers and sisters?"

Without missing a beat one little boy answered, "Thou shall not kill."

Your Noisy World

Be silent before the Lord and wait expectantly for Him.

Psalm 37:7 HCSB

Face it: We live in a noisy world, a world filled with distractions, frustrations, and complications. But if we allow those distractions to separate us from God's peace, we do ourselves a profound disservice.

Are you one of those busy women who rush through the day with scarcely a single moment for quiet contemplation and prayer? If so, it's time to reorder your priorities.

Nothing is more important than the time you spend with your Savior. So be still and claim the inner peace that is your spiritual birthright: the peace of Jesus Christ. It is offered freely; it has been paid for in full; it is yours for the asking. So ask. And then share.

Jesus taught us by example to get out of the rat race and recharge our batteries.

Barbara Johnson

REAL INSIGHTS

The manifold rewards of a serious, consistent prayer life demonstrate clearly that time with our Lord should be our first priority.

Shirley Dobson

The Lord Jesus, available to people much of the time, left them, sometimes a great while before day, to go up to the hills where He could commune in solitude with His Father.

Elisabeth Elliot

SMILE!

So far today, God, I've done all right. I haven't gossiped; I haven't lost my temper; I haven't been greedy, grumpy, nasty, selfish, or over-indulgent. I'm really glad about that. But in a few minutes, Lord, I'm going to get out of bed and from then on, I'm probably going to need a lot more help. Thank You. In Jesus' name . . . amen

THOUGHT FOR TODAY:
MORNING PRAISE WILL MAKE YOUR DAYS.

When Mistakes Are Made

Therefore, if anyone is in Christ, he is a new creation;
the old has gone, the new has come!

2 Corinthians 5:17 NIV

Mistakes: nobody likes 'em but everybody makes 'em. Sometimes, even if you're a very good person, you're going to mess things up. And when you do, God is always ready to forgive you—He'll do His part, but you should be willing to do your part, too. Here's what you need to do:

1. If you've been engaging in behavior that is against the will of God, cease and desist (that means stop).

2. If you made a mistake, learn from it and don't repeat it (that's called getting smarter).

3. If you've hurt somebody, apologize and ask for forgiveness (that's called doing the right thing).

4. Ask for God's forgiveness, too (He'll give it whenever you ask, but you do need to ask!).

Have you made a mistake? If so, today is the perfect day to make things right with everybody (and the word "everybody" includes yourself, your family, your friends, and your God).

Mistakes are the price you pay for being human; repeated mistakes are the price you pay for being stubborn. So don't be hardheaded: learn from your experiences—the first time!

At the end of their first date, a young man took his favorite girl home. Emboldened by the night, he decided to try for that important first kiss. With an air of confidence, he leaned with his hand against the wall and, smiling, said, "Darling, how about a goodnight kiss?"

Horrified, she replied, "Are you mad? My parents will see us!"

"Oh come on! Who's gonna see us at this hour?"

"No, please. Can you imagine if we get caught?"

"Oh come on, there's nobody around; they're all sleeping," he continued selling.

"No way," she replied. "It's just too risky!"

"Oh please, please, I like you so much!"

"No, no, and no. I like you, too, but I just can't!"

"Oh yes you can. Please?"

"No. I just can't."

"Pleeeeease?..."

Out of the blue, the porch light turned on, and the girl's big sister showed up in her pajamas. In a sleepy voice the sister said, "Dad says to go ahead and give him a kiss. Or I can do it. Or if need be, Dad says he'll come down and kiss the boy himself. But for crying out loud, tell that boy to take his hand off the intercom button!"

Wise Yet?

Do you want to be counted wise, to build a reputation
for wisdom? Here's what you do:
Live well, live wisely, live humbly.
It's the way you live, not the way you talk, that counts.

James 3:13 MSG

Are you a wise woman? And, are you becoming a little wiser every day? Hopefully so. All of us would like to be wise, but not all of us are willing to do the work that is required to become wise. Why? Because wisdom isn't free—it takes time and effort to acquire.

To become wise, we must seek God's wisdom and live according to His Word. To become wise, we must seek wisdom with consistency and purpose. To become wise, we must not only learn the lessons of the Christian life, we must also live by them.

If you sincerely desire to become wise—and if you seek to share your hard-earned wisdom with others—your actions must give credence to your words. The best way to share one's wisdom—perhaps the only way—is not by words, but by example.

Wisdom is like a savings account: If you add to it consistently, then eventually you'll have a great sum. The secret to success is consistency. Do you seek wisdom? Then seek it every day, and seek it in the right place. That place, of course, is, first and foremost, the Word of God.

REAL INSIGHTS

No matter how many books you read, no matter how many schools you attend, you're never really wise until you start making wise choices.

Marie T. Freeman

Wisdom is knowledge applied. Head knowledge is useless on the battlefield. Knowledge stamped on the heart makes one wise.

Beth Moore

A young boy had just gotten his driving permit. He asked his father, who was a minister, if they could discuss the use of the car. His father took him to his study and said to him, "I'll make a deal with you. You bring your grades up, study your Bible, and get your hair cut, and we'll talk about it."

After about a month the boy came back and again asked his father if they could discuss using the car. They again went to the father's study where his father said, "Son, I've been real proud of you. You have brought your grades up, you've studied your Bible diligently, but you didn't get your hair cut!" The young man waited a minute and replied, "You know, Dad, I've been thinking about that. You know, Samson had long hair, Moses had long hair, why even Jesus had long hair." To which his father replied, "Yes, and they WALKED everywhere they went!"

The Hem of His Garment

Now faith is being sure of what we hope for and certain of what we do not see.

Hebrews 11:1 NIV

A suffering woman sought healing in an unusual way: she simply touched the hem of Jesus' garment. When she did, Jesus turned and said, "Daughter, be of good comfort; thy faith hath made thee whole" (Matthew 9:22 KJV). We, too, can be made whole when we place our faith completely and unwaveringly in the person of Jesus Christ.

Concentration camp survivor Corrie ten Boom relied on faith during ten months of imprisonment and torture. Later, despite the fact that four of her family members had died in Nazi death camps, Corrie's faith was unshaken. She wrote, "There is no pit so deep that God's love is not deeper still." Christians take note: Genuine faith in God means faith in all circumstances, happy or sad, joyful or tragic.

When you place your faith, your trust, indeed your life in the hands of Christ Jesus, you'll be amazed at the marvelous things He can do with you and through you. So strengthen your faith through praise, through worship, through Bible study, and through prayer. Then, trust God's plans. Your Heavenly Father is standing at the door of your heart. If you reach out to Him in faith, He will give you peace and heal your broken spirit. Be content to touch even the smallest fragment of the Master's garment, and He will make you whole.

REAL INSIGHTS

If God chooses to remain silent, faith is content.

Ruth Bell Graham

Faith does not concern itself with the entire journey. One step is enough.

Mrs. Charles E. Cowman

A nun who worked for a local home health care agency was out making her rounds when she ran out of gas. As luck would have it, there was a gas station just down the street. She walked to the station to borrow a can with enough gas to get her car started, but the attendant regretfully told her that the only can he owned had just been loaned out. So the nun walked back to her car to see if she could find something to hold a few ounces of that precious petrol.

After looking through her car for something to carry to the filling station, she spotted a bedpan that she was taking to her patient. Always resourceful, the nun carried the bedpan back to the station, filled it with gasoline, and carefully carried it back to her car. As she was pouring the gas into her tank, two men walked by. One of them turned to the other and said, "Now that's what I call faith!"

To Shop or Not to Shop?

No one can serve two masters.
The person will hate one master and love the other,
or will follow one master and refuse to follow the other.
You cannot serve both God and worldly riches.

Matthew 6:24 NCV

Is "shop till you drop" your motto? Hopefully not! On the grand stage of a well-lived life, material possessions should play a rather small role. Of course, we all need the basic necessities of life, but once we meet those needs, the piling up of stuff creates more problems than it solves.

Our society is in love with money and the things that money can buy. God is not. God cares about people, not possessions, and so must we. We must, to the best of our abilities, love our neighbors as ourselves, and we must, to the best of our abilities, resist the mighty temptation to place possessions ahead of people.

How much stuff is too much stuff? Well, if your desire for stuff is getting in the way of your desire to know God, then you've got too much stuff—it's as simple as that.

If you find yourself wrapped up in the concerns of the material world, it's time to reorder your priorities by turning your thoughts to more important matters. And, it's time to begin storing up riches that will endure throughout eternity: the spiritual kind. Money, in and of itself, is not evil; worshipping money is. So today, as you prioritize matters of importance in your life, remember that God is almighty, but the dollar is not.

REAL INSIGHTS

As faithful stewards of what we have, ought we not to give earnest thought to our staggering surplus?

Elisabeth Elliot

We own too many things that aren't worth owning.

Marie T. Freeman

A woman was taking it easy, lying on the grass and looking up at the clouds. She was identifying shapes when she decided to talk to God.

"God," she said, "how long is a million years?"

God answered, "In my frame of reference, it's about a minute."

The woman asked, "God, how much is a million dollars?"

God answered, "To Me, it's a penny."

The woman then asked, "God, can I have a penny?"

God said, "In a minute."

Doing It Now

If you do nothing in a difficult time, your strength is limited.

Proverbs 24:10 HCSB

When something important needs to be done, the best time to do it is sooner rather than later. But sometimes, instead of doing the smart thing (which, by the way, is choosing "sooner"), we may choose "later." When we do, we may pay a heavy price for our shortsightedness.

The habit of procrastination takes a two-fold toll on its victims. First, important work goes unfinished; second (and more importantly), valuable energy is wasted in the process of putting off the things that remain undone. Procrastination results from an individual's short-sighted attempt to postpone temporary discomfort. What results is a senseless cycle of 1. Delay, followed by 2. Worry followed by 3. A panicky and futile attempt to "catch up." Procrastination is, at its core, a struggle against oneself; the only antidote is action.

Once you acquire the habit of doing what needs to be done when it needs to be done, you will avoid untold trouble, worry, and stress. So learn to defeat procrastination by paying less attention to your fears and more attention to your responsibilities.

Are you one of those people who puts things off till the last minute? If so, it's time to change your ways. Whatever "it" is, do it now. When you do, you won't have to worry about "it" later.

REAL INSIGHTS

Never fail to do something because you don't feel like it. Sometimes you just have to do it now, and you'll feel like it later.

Marie T. Freeman

Do noble things, do not dream them all day long.

Charles Kingsley

CHURCH BULLETIN BLOOPERS

Ladies, don't forget the rummage sale.
It's a chance to get rid of those things not worth keeping around the house. Don't forget your husbands.

Please place your donation in the envelope along with the deceased person you want remembered.

The peacemaking meeting scheduled for today has been canceled due to a conflict.

God Can Handle It

For I, the Lord your God, hold your right hand and say to you:
Do not fear, I will help you.

Isaiah 41:13 HCSB

Because we are imperfect human beings living imperfect lives, we worry. Even though we, as Christians, have the assurance of salvation—even though we, as believers, have the promise of God's love and protection—we find ourselves fretting over the countless details of everyday life. Jesus understood our concerns, and He addressed them.

In the 6th chapter of Matthew, Jesus makes it clear that the heart of God is a protective, caring heart:

Therefore I say to you, do not worry about your life, what you will eat or what you will drink; nor about your body, what you will put on. Is not life more than food and the body more than clothing? Look at the birds of the air, for they neither sow nor reap nor gather into barns; yet your heavenly Father feeds them. Are you not of more value than they? Which of you by worrying can add one cubit to his stature? . . . Therefore do not worry about tomorrow, for tomorrow will worry about its own things. Sufficient for the day is its own trouble.
(vv. 25-27, 34)

Perhaps you are uncertain about your future, your finances, your relationships, or your health. Or perhaps you are simply a "worrier" by nature. If so, make Matthew 6 a regular part of your daily Bible reading. This beautiful passage will remind you that God still sits in His heaven and you are His beloved child. Then, perhaps, you will worry a little less and trust God a little more, and that's as it should be because God is trustworthy . . . and you are protected.

God is always sufficient in perfect proportion to our need.

Beth Moore

One day a group of eminent scientists got together and decided that man had come a long way and no longer needed God. So they picked one scientist to go and tell God that they were finished with Him. The scientist walked up to God and said, "Sir, we've decided that we no longer need You. We can now clone people, and we can do lots more amazing things. So why don't You just retire?"

God listened patiently to the scientist and then said, "Very well, but first, how about this: let's have a Man-making contest."

The scientist replied, "That's great!" But God added, "Now, we're going to do this just like I did back in the old days with Adam." The scientist said, "Sure, no problem," as he bent down and grabbed a handful of dirt. God just looked at him and said, "No, no, no. Go get your own dirt!"

You and Your Conscience

So I strive always to keep my conscience clear before God and man.

Acts 24:16 NIV

It has been said that character is what we are when nobody is watching. How true. When we do things that we know aren't right, we try to hide them from our families and friends. But even then, God is watching.

Few things in life torment us more than a guilty conscience. And, few things in life provide more contentment than the knowledge that we are obeying the conscience that God has placed in our hearts.

If you sincerely want to create the best possible life for yourself and your loved ones, never forsake your conscience. And remember this: when you walk with God, your character will take care of itself . . . and you won't need to look over your shoulder to see who, besides God, is watching.

REAL INSIGHTS

God desires that we become spiritually healthy enough through faith to have a conscience that rightly interprets the work of the Holy Spirit.

Beth Moore

If I am walking along the street with a very disfiguring hole in the back of my dress, of which I am in ignorance, it is certainly a very great comfort to me to have a kind friend who will tell me of it. And similarly, it is indeed a comfort to know that there is always abiding with me a divine, all-seeing Comforter, who will reprove me for all my faults and will not let me go on in a fatal unconsciousness of them.

Hannah Whitall Smith

COMING SOON TO A CHURCH SIGN NEAR YOU . . .

NO JESUS, NO PEACE;
KNOW JESUS, KNOW PEACE!

THE BREAD OF LIFE NEVER GETS STALE.

HEAVENLY FORECAST:
JESUS WILL REIGN FOREVER!

Beyond Discouragement

But as for you, be strong; don't be discouraged,
for your work has a reward.

2 Chronicles 15:7 HCSB

We Christians have many reasons to celebrate. God is in His heaven; Christ has risen, and we are the sheep of His flock. Yet sometimes, even the most devout Christian women can become discouraged. After all, we live in a world where expectations can be high and demands can be even higher. If you become discouraged with the direction of your day or your life, turn your thoughts and prayers to God. He is a God of possibility, not negativity. He will help you count your blessings instead of your hardships. And then, with a renewed spirit of optimism and hope, you can properly thank your Father in heaven for His blessings, for His love, and for His Son.

REAL INSIGHTS

Overcoming discouragement is simply a matter of taking away the DIS and adding the EN.

Barbara Johnson

Working in the vineyard, working all the day, never be discouraged, only watch and pray.

Fanny Crosby

God does not dispense strength and encouragement like a druggist fills your prescription. The Lord doesn't promise to give us something to take so we can handle our weary moments. He promises us Himself. That is all. And that is enough.

Charles Swindoll

CHURCH BULLETIN BLOOPERS

Next Thursday there will be tryouts for the choir.
They need all the help they can get.

Don't let worry kill you. Let the Church help.

Thursday night will be a potluck supper.
Prayer and medication to follow.

Real Repentance

Come back to the LORD and live!

Amos 5:6 NLT

Who among us has sinned? All of us. But, God calls upon us to turn away from sin by following His commandments. And the good news is this: When we do ask God's forgiveness and turn our hearts to Him, He forgives us absolutely and completely.

Genuine repentance requires more than simply offering God apologies for our misdeeds. Real repentance may start with feelings of sorrow and remorse, but it ends only when we turn away from the sin that has heretofore distanced us from our Creator. In truth, we offer our most meaningful apologies to God not with our words, but with our actions. As long as we are still engaged in sin, we may be "repenting," but we have not fully "repented."

Is there an aspect of your life that is distancing you from your God? If so, ask for His forgiveness, and—just as importantly—stop sinning. Then, wrap yourself in the protection of God's Word. When you do, you will be secure.

To do so no more is the truest repentance.

Martin Luther

A painter was painting a church steeple on a very hot day. The painter was about half way down and, as the steeple widened out, it was taking more paint.

The painter felt that he might not have enough paint to finish, but he was hot and tired, and he didn't want to make another trip to the ground, so he decided to stretch the paint by adding thinner.

When finished, he lowered himself to the ground and went about cleaning up. Then he looked up to see the results of his work and noted that the area with the thinned paint looked decidedly different.

He was pondering about what to do when the sky turned dark, lightning flashed and a loud thunderclap nearly knocked him off his feet. Then, in a booming voice from the sky came the words, "REPAINT AND THIN NO MORE!"

On Sad Days

Why am I so depressed? Why this turmoil within me?
Put your hope in God, for I will still praise Him,
my Savior and my God.

Psalm 42:11 HCSB

Some days are light and happy, and some days are not. When we face the inevitable dark days of life, we must choose how we will respond. Will we allow ourselves to sink even more deeply into our own sadness, or will we do the difficult work of pulling ourselves out? We bring light to the dark days of life by turning first to God, and then to trusted family members and friends. Then, we must go to work solving the problems that confront us. When we do, the clouds will eventually part, and the sun will shine once more upon our souls.

When life is difficult, God wants us to have a faith that trusts and waits.

Kay Arthur

REAL LIFE DEVOTIONS AND FUNNY STORIES FOR WOMEN

REAL INSIGHTS

God is good, and heaven is forever. These two facts should brighten up even the darkest day.

Marie T. Freeman

The strengthening of faith comes from staying with it in the hour of trial. We should not shrink from tests of faith.

Catherine Marshall

SMILE!

Joe was opening a new business, and one of his friends decided to send flowers for the occasion.

The flowers arrived and Joe read the card. It said, "Rest in Peace." Joe, enraged, called the florist to complain.

The florist replied, "Sir, I'm really sorry for the mistake, but if you think you've got it bad, remember that somewhere in this county, there's a funeral taking place today, and they have flowers with a note saying, "Congratulations on your new location."

God Is Love

God is love, and the one who remains in love remains in God, and God remains in him.

1 John 4:16 HCSB

The words of 1 John 4:8 teach us that "He who does not love does not know God, for God is love" (NKJV). And because we can be assured that God is love, we can also be assured that God's heart is a loving heart.

God loves you. He loves you more than you can imagine; His affection is deeper than you can fathom. God made you in His own image and gave you salvation through the person of His Son Jesus Christ. And as a result, you have an important decision to make. You must decide what to do about God's love: you can return it . . . or not.

When you accept the love that flows from the heart of God, you are transformed. When you embrace God's love, you feel differently about yourself, your neighbors, your community, your church, and your world. When you open your heart to God's love, you will feel compelled to share God's message—and His compassion—with others.

God's heart is overflowing with love . . . for you. Accept that love. Return that love. And share that love. Today.

REAL INSIGHTS

I can tell you, from personal experience of walking with God for over fifty years, that He is the Lover of my soul.

Vonette Bright

God loves these people, too, just because they're unattractive or warped in their thinking doesn't mean the Lord doesn't love them.

Ruth Bell Graham

Let God have you, and let God love you—and don't be surprised if your heart begins to hear music you've never heard and your feet learn to dance as never before.

Max Lucado

COMING SOON TO A CHURCH SIGN NEAR YOU ...

GOD LOVES PEOPLE—
IN FACT HE SENT HIS SON TO BE ONE!

GOD LOVES YOU
WHETHER YOU LIKE IT OR NOT.

GRIN! GOD LOVES YOU!
THE REST OF US WILL WONDER
WHAT YOU'VE BEEN UP TO.

Obedience Now

For God is working in you, giving you the desire to obey him and the power to do what pleases him.

Philippians 2:13 NLT

Obedience to God is determined, not by words, but by deeds. Talking about righteousness is easy; living righteously is far more difficult, especially in today's temptation-filled world.

Since God created Adam and Eve, we human beings have been rebelling against our Creator. Why? Because we are unwilling to trust God's Word, and we are unwilling to follow His commandments. God has given us a guidebook for righteous living called the Holy Bible. It contains thorough instructions which, if followed, lead to fulfillment, righteousness, and salvation. But, if we choose to ignore God's commandments, the results are as predictable as they are tragic.

Unless we are willing to abide by God's laws, all of our righteous proclamations ring hollow. How can we best proclaim our love for the Lord? By obeying Him. And, for further instructions, read the manual.

REAL INSIGHTS

God is God. Because He is God, He is worthy of my trust and obedience. I will find rest nowhere but in His holy will, a will that is unspeakably beyond my largest notions of what He is up to.

Elisabeth Elliot

The pathway of obedience can sometimes be difficult, but it always leads to a strengthening of our inner woman.

Vonette Bright

A Sunday school teacher was carefully explaining the story of Elijah the Prophet and the false prophets of Baal. She explained how Elijah, being obedient to God, built an altar, put wood upon it, cut the steer in pieces, and laid the pieces upon the altar. Next, Elijah commanded the people of God to fill four barrels of water and pour it over the altar. He had them do this four times.

"Now," said the teacher, "can anyone in the class tell me why the Lord would have Elijah pour water over the steer on the altar?"

A little boy in the back of the room started waving his hand. "I know! I know!" he said. "To make the gravy!"

Walking with the Wise

Listen to advice and accept correction,
and in the end you will be wise.

Proverbs 19:20 NCV

Do you wish to become wise? Then you must walk with people who, by their words and their presence, make you wiser. And, to the best of your ability, you must avoid those people who encourage you to think foolish thoughts or do foolish things.

Today, as a gift to yourself, select, from your friends and family members, a mentor whose judgement you trust. Then listen carefully to your mentor's advice and be willing to accept that advice, even if accepting it requires effort or pain, or both. Consider your mentor to be God's gift to you. Thank God for that gift, and use it.

No matter how crazy or nutty your life has seemed, God can make something strong and good out of it. He can help you grow wide branches for others to use as shelter.

Barbara Johnson

REAL INSIGHT

It takes a wise person to give good advice, but an even wiser person to take it.

Marie T. Freeman

GETTING TO KNOW THE TATE FAMILY

Do you know how many members of the Tate family belong to your church? There is old man Dic-Tate who wants to run everything, while Uncle Ro-Tate tries to change everything. There's sister Agi-Tate who stirs up plenty of trouble, with help from her husband, Irri-Tate.

Whenever new projects are suggested, Hesi-Tate and his wife, Vege-Tate, want to wait until next year. Then there is Aunt Imi-Tate, who wants our church to be like all the others. Devas-Tate provides the voice of doom, while Poten-Tate wants to be a big shot.

But not all members of the family are bad. Brother Facili-Tate is quite helpful in church matters. And a delightful, happy member of the family is Miss Felici-Tate. Cousins Cogi-Tate and Medi-Tate always thinks things over and lend helpful, steady hands. And of course there is the white sheep of the family, Ampu-Tate, who has completely cut himself off from the church.

How about it—do you know anyone in the Tate family?

God First

Let us fix our eyes on Jesus, the author and perfecter of our faith, who for the joy set before him endured the cross, scorning its shame, and sat down at the right hand of the throne of God.

Hebrews 12:2 NIV

"First things first." These words are easy to speak but hard to put into practice. For busy women living in a demanding world, placing first things first can be difficult indeed. Why? Because so many people are expecting so many things from us!

If you're having trouble prioritizing your day, perhaps you've been trying to organize your life according to your own plans, not God's. A better strategy, of course, is to take your daily obligations and place them in the hands of the One who created you. To do so, you must prioritize your day according to God's commandments, and you must seek His will and His wisdom in all matters. Then, you can face the day with the assurance that the same God who created our universe out of nothingness will help you place first things first in your own life.

Do you feel overwhelmed or confused? Turn the concerns of this day over to God—prayerfully, earnestly, and often. Then listen for His answer . . . and trust the answer He gives.

The manifold rewards of a serious, consistent prayer life demonstrate clearly that time with our Lord should be our first priority.

Shirley Dobson

We set our eyes on the finish line, forgetting the past, and straining toward the mark of spiritual maturity and fruitfulness.

Vonette Bright

Two men were shipwrecked on a deserted island. The instant they waded up on shore, one of them started screaming, "We're going to die! We're going to die! There's no food! No water! We're going to die!"

The second man was propped up against a palm tree and acting so calmly it drove the first man crazy. "Don't you understand? We're going to die!!" the first man said. But the second man said, "No, you don't understand. I make $100,000 a week."

The first man looked at him quite dumbfounded and asked, "What difference does it make? We're on an island with no food and no water! We're going to die!!!"

The second man answered, "You just don't get it. I make $100,000 a week, and I tithe. My pastor will find me!"

The Beauty of Humility

*For everyone who exalts himself will be humbled,
and the one who humbles himself will be exalted.*

Luke 14:11 HCSB

Humility is not, in most cases, a naturally occurring human trait. Most of us, it seems, are more than willing to overestimate our own accomplishments. We are tempted to say, "Look how wonderful I am!" . . . hoping all the while that the world will agree with our own self-appraisals.

God honors humility . . . and He rewards those who humbly serve Him. When we acquire the wisdom to be humble, we bring enlightenment to the world (and blessings to ourselves).

But if we cannot overcome the tendency to overestimate our own accomplishments, then God still has some important lessons to teach us—lessons about the wisdom, the power, and the beauty of humility.

If you know who you are in Christ, your personal ego is not an issue.

Beth Moore

We are never stronger than the moment we admit we are weak.

Beth Moore

Humility is the fairest and rarest flower that blooms.

Charles Swindoll

Bobby Bowden, the coaching legend at Florida State University, told of a humbling experience. He and his wife traveled to a small town in New England to try and get away from it all. They were hopeful they would be able to move about without too much recognition and enjoy some solitude.

One afternoon they went to a movie. They entered the theater and noticed several other couples. As they made their way to their seats there was a smattering of applause. Bobby raised his hand and acknowledged the recognition.

After the movie, one of the patrons approached Coach Bowden and said, "You may not know why we were applauding you when you entered the theater. The fact is that they won't start the movie here until a minimum number of people show up. And you got us over the minimum!"

Coach Bowden acknowledged that God has His own ways of keeping us humble.

Discipline and Life

Discipline yourself for the purpose of godliness.

1 Timothy 4:7 NASB

Wise women understand the importance of discipline. In Proverbs 28:19, the message is clear: "Those who work their land will have plenty of food, but the ones who chase empty dreams instead will end up poor" (NCV).

If we work diligently and faithfully, we can expect a bountiful harvest. But we must never expect the harvest to precede the labor.

Poet Mary Frances Butts advised, "Build a little fence of trust around today. Fill each space with loving work, and therein stay." And her words still apply.

Thoughtful women understand that God doesn't reward laziness or misbehavior. To the contrary, God expects His children (of all ages) to lead disciplined lives . . . and when they do, He rewards them.

As we seek to become disciples of Jesus Christ, we should never forget that the word *disciple* is directly related to the word *discipline*. To be a disciple of the Lord Jesus Christ is to know his discipline.

Dennis Swanberg

REAL INSIGHTS

Discipline is training that develops and corrects.

Charles Stanley

The Bible calls for discipline and a recognition of authority. Children must learn this at home.

Billy Graham

MODERN CHURCH: CHRISTIAN-LITE

Has the heaviness of your old-fashioned church got you weighted down? Try us! We are the New and Improved Lite Church of the Valley. Studies have shown we have 24% fewer commitments than other churches. We guarantee to trim off guilt, because we are Low-Cal: Low Calvin, that is. We are the home of the 7.5% tithe.

We promise 35-minute worship services, with 7-minute sermons. Next Sunday's exciting text is the story of the Feeding of the 500.

We have only 6 Commandments—your choice! We use just 3 gospels in our contemporary New Testament "Good Sound Bites for Modern Human Beings."

We take the offering every other week; all major credit cards accepted.

We are looking forward with great anticipation to our 800-year Millennium.

Yes, the New and Improved Lite Church of the Valley could be just what you are looking for. We are everything you want in a church . . . and less!

Courtesy According to God

Are there those among you who are truly wise and understanding? Then they should show it by living right and doing good things with a gentleness that comes from wisdom.

James 3:13 NCV

Does the Bible instruct us in matters of etiquette and courtesy? Of course it does. The words of Matthew 7:12 are clear: "In everything, therefore, treat people the same way you want them to treat you, for this is the Law and the Prophets" (NASB).

The Bible doesn't instruct, "In some things, treat people as you wish to be treated." And, it doesn't say, "From time to time, treat others with kindness." The Bible instructs us to treat others as we wish to be treated in every aspect of our daily lives.

Today try to be a little kinder than necessary to family members, friends, and total strangers. And as you consider all the things God has done for you, honor Him with your kind words and good deeds. He deserves no less, and neither do your loved ones.

REAL INSIGHT

Courtesy is contagious.

Marie T. Freeman

When you extend hospitality to others, you're not trying to impress people; you're trying to reflect God to them.

Max Lucado

Only the courteous can love, but it is love that makes them courteous.

C. S. Lewis

SMILE!

"I hope you didn't take it personally, Reverend," the embarrassed woman said after a church service, "when my husband walked out during your sermon."

"I did find it rather disconcerting," the preacher replied.

"It's not a reflection on you, sir," she insisted. "Cecil has been walking in his sleep ever since he was a child."

A Happy Christian

But happy are those . . .
whose hope is in the LORD their God.

Psalm 146:5 NLT

Happiness depends less upon our circumstances than upon our thoughts. When we turn our thoughts to God, to His gifts, and to His glorious creation, we experience the joy that God intends for His children. But, when we focus on the negative aspects of life, we suffer needlessly.

Do you sincerely want to be a happy Christian? Then set your mind and your heart upon God's love and His grace. The fullness of life in Christ is available to all who seek it and claim it. Count yourself among that number. Seek first the salvation that is available through a personal relationship with Jesus Christ, and then claim the joy, the peace, and the spiritual abundance that the Shepherd offers His sheep.

REAL INSIGHTS

I became aware of one very important concept I had missed before: my attitude—not my circumstances—was what was making me unhappy.

Vonette Bright

I am truly happy with Jesus Christ. I couldn't live without Him.

Ruth Bell Graham

Christ is the secret, the source, the substance, the center, and the circumference of all true and lasting gladness.

Mrs. Charles E. Cowman

COMING SOON TO A CHURCH SIGN NEAR YOU . . .

SMILE—
IT INCREASES YOUR FACE VALUE.

GOD MADE ROUND FACES;
MAN MAKES 'EM LONG.

HAPPINESS,
LIKE ITS OPPOSITE,
IS HABIT-FORMING.

No More Gossip!

Though some tongues just love the taste of gossip,
Christians have better uses for language than that.
Don't talk dirty or silly. That kind of talk doesn't fit our style.
Thanksgiving is our dialect.

Ephesians 5:4 MSG

Face it: gossip is bad—and the Bible clearly tells us that gossip is wrong.

When we say things that we don't want other people to know we said, we're being somewhat dishonest, but if the things we say aren't true, we're being very dishonest. Either way, we have done something that we may regret later, especially when the other person finds out.

So do yourself a big favor: don't gossip. It's a waste of words, and it's the wrong thing to do. Besides, you'll feel better about yourself if you don't gossip . . . and other people will feel better about you, too.

REAL INSIGHTS

Never utter in your neighbor's absence what you wouldn't say in his presence.

Mary Magdalene di Pazzi

Change the heart, and you change the speech.

Warren Wiersbe

When you talk, choose the very same words that you would use if Jesus were looking over your shoulder. Because He is.

Marie T. Freeman

COMING SOON TO A CHURCH SIGN NEAR YOU . . .

TO BELITTLE IS TO BE LITTLE.

AT THE HEART OF SIN IS THE LETTER "I".

IN THE DARK? FOLLOW THE SON.

Richly Blessed

Blessings are on the head of the righteous.

Proverbs 10:6 HCSB

Have you counted your blessings lately? You should. Of course, God's gifts are too numerous to count, but as a grateful Christian, you should attempt to count them nonetheless.

Your blessings include life, family, friends, talents, and possessions, for starters. And your greatest gift—a treasure that was paid for on the cross and is yours for the asking—is God's gift of salvation through Christ Jesus.

As believing Christians, we have all been blessed beyond measure. Thus, thanksgiving should become a habit, a regular part of our daily routines. Today, let us pause and thank our Creator for His blessings. And let us demonstrate our gratitude to the Giver of all things good by using His gifts for the glory of His kingdom.

God's love for His children is unconditional, no strings attached. But, God's blessings on our lives do come with a condition—obedience. If we are to receive the fullness of God's blessings, we must obey Him and keep His commandments.

Jim Gallery

God is always far more willing to give us good things than we are anxious to have them.

Catherine Marshall

The Christian life is motivated, not by a list of do's and don'ts, but by the gracious outpouring of God's love and blessing.

Anne Graham Lotz

A country preacher decided to skip services one Sunday and head to the hills to do some bear hunting. As he rounded the corner on a perilous twist in the trail, he and a bear collided, sending him and his rifle tumbling down the mountainside. Before he knew it, the rifle went one way and he went the other, landing on a rock and breaking both legs. That was the good news. The bad news was the ferocious bear was charging at him from a distance, and he couldn't move.

"Oh Lord," the preacher prayed, "I'm so sorry for skipping services today to come out here and hunt. Please forgive me and grant me just one wish: please make a Christian out of that bear that's coming at me. Please, Lord!"

That very instant, the bear skidded to a halt, fell to its knees, clasped its paws together, and began to pray aloud right at the preacher's feet. "Dear Lord, bless this food I am about to receive . . . in Jesus' name . . . Amen."

God's Guidance

*The LORD says, "I will guide you along the best pathway
for your life. I will advise you and watch over you."*

Psalm 32:8 NLT

The Bible promises that God will guide you if you let Him. Your job, of course, is to let Him. But sometimes, you will be tempted to do otherwise. Sometimes, you'll be tempted to go along with the crowd; other times, you'll be tempted to do things your way, not God's way. When you feel those temptations, resist them.

What will you allow to guide you through the coming day: your own desires (or, for that matter, the desires of your friends)? Or will you allow God to lead the way? The answer should be obvious. You should let God be your guide. When you entrust your life to Him completely and without reservation, God will give you the strength to meet any challenge, the courage to face any trial, and the wisdom to live in His righteousness. So trust Him today and seek His guidance. When you do, your next step will be the right one.

REAL LIFE DEVOTIONS AND FUNNY STORIES FOR WOMEN

REAL INSIGHTS

If we neglect the Bible, we cannot expect to benefit from the wisdom and direction that result from knowing God's Word.

Vonette Bright

It is a joy that God never abandons His children. He guides faithfully all who listen to His directions.

Corrie ten Boom

We must always invite Jesus to be the navigator of our plans, desires, wills, and emotions, for He is the way, the truth, and the life.

Bill Bright

COMING SOON TO A CHURCH SIGN NEAR YOU ...

IF GOD IS YOUR CO-PILOT . . .
SWAP SEATS!

IS GOD YOUR SPARE WHEEL
OR YOUR STEERING WHEEL?

WE SET THE SAIL;
GOD MAKES THE WIND.

Too Busy?

Careful planning puts you ahead in the long run;
hurry and scurry puts you further behind.

Proverbs 21:5 MSG

Everybody knows you're a very busy woman. But here's a question: are you able to squeeze time into your hectic schedule for God? Hopefully so! But if you're one of those girls who rush through the day with scarcely a single moment to talk with your Creator, it's time to reshuffle your priorities.

You live in a noisy world, a world filled with distractions, frustrations, temptations, and complications. But if you allow the distractions of everyday life to distract you from God's peace, you're doing yourself a big disservice. So here's some good advice: instead of rushing nonstop through the day, slow yourself down long enough to have a few quiet minutes with God.

Nothing is more important than the time you spend with your Heavenly Father. Absolutely nothing. So be still and claim the inner peace that is your spiritual birthright: the peace of Jesus Christ. It is offered freely; it has been paid for in full; it is yours for the asking. So ask. And then share.

REAL INSIGHTS

The demand of every day kept me so busy that I subconsciously equated my busyness with commitment to Christ.

Vonette Bright

Frustration is not the will of God. There is time to do anything and everything that God wants us to do.

Elisabeth Elliot

In our tense, uptight society where folks are rushing to make appointments they have already missed, a good laugh can be as refreshing as a cup of cold water in the desert.

Barbara Johnson

COMING SOON TO A CHURCH SIGN NEAR YOU ...

THE RAPTURE:
IT'S THE ONLY WAY TO FLY!

THE RAPTURE IS COMING . . .
GET RIGHT OR GET LEFT!

Beyond Guilt

*There is therefore now no condemnation to those
who are in Christ Jesus, who do not walk according
to the flesh, but according to the Spirit.*

Romans 8:1 NKJV

All of us have made mistakes. Sometimes our failures result from our own shortsightedness. On other occasions, we are swept up in events that are beyond our abilities to control. Under either set of circumstances, we may experience intense feelings of guilt. But God has an answer for the guilt that we feel. That answer, of course, is His forgiveness.

When we ask our Heavenly Father for His forgiveness, He forgives us completely and without reservation. Then, we must do the difficult work of forgiving ourselves in the same way that God has forgiven us: thoroughly and unconditionally.

If you're feeling guilty, then it's time for a special kind of housecleaning—a housecleaning of your mind and your heart . . . beginning NOW!

REAL INSIGHTS

If God has forgiven you, why can't you forgive yourself?

Marie T. Freeman

Identify the sin. Confess it. Turn from it. Avoid it at all costs. Live with a clean, forgiven conscience. Don't dwell on what God has forgotten!

Max Lucado

NOW AVAILABLE!

Revised Gospel Hymns for Today's Generation
of Modern Churchgoers.
Now the Old Favorites Can Be Sung Without Guilt,
Discomfort, Conviction, or Political Incorrectness.
Titles Included:

"Amazing Grace, How Interesting the Sound"
"Pillow of Ages, Fluffed for Me"
"What an Acquaintance We Have in Jesus"
"Blessed Insurance"
"I Surrender Some"
"Onward Social Workers"
"Standing on the Premises"
"Sweet Minute of Prayer"
And the All-Time Children's Classic:
"I Love Me, This I Know"

Finding Hope

*Now may the God of hope fill you with all joy
and peace in believing, so that you may overflow
with hope by the power of the Holy Spirit.*

Romans 15:13 HCSB

There are few sadder sights on earth than the sight of a woman who has lost hope. In difficult times, hope can be elusive, but those who place their faith in God's promises need never lose it. After all, God is good; His love endures; He has promised His children the gift of eternal life. And, God keeps His promises.

Despite God's promises, despite Christ's love, and despite our countless blessings, we're only human, and we can still lose hope from time to time. When we do, we need the encouragement of Christian friends, the life-changing power of prayer, and the healing truth of God's Holy Word.

If you find yourself falling into the spiritual traps of worry and discouragement, seek the healing touch of Jesus and the encouraging words of fellow believers. And if you find a friend in need, remind him or her of the peace that is found through a genuine relationship with Christ.

This world can be a place of trials and troubles, but as believers, we are secure. God has promised us peace, joy, and eternal life. And, of course, God keeps His promises today, tomorrow, and forever.

REAL INSIGHTS

Hope must be in the future tense. Faith, to be faith, must always be in the present tense.

Catherine Marshall

Love is the seed of all hope. It is the enticement to trust, to risk, to try, and to go on.

Gloria Gaither

I discovered that sorrow was not to be feared but rather endured with hope and expectancy that God would use it to visit and bless my life.

Jill Briscoe

CHURCH BULLETIN BLOOPERS

Remember in prayer the many who are sick
of our church and the community.

Weight Watchers will meet at 7 PM in the sanctuary.
Please use large double door at the side entrance.

His Joy and Yours

A joyful heart is good medicine,
but a broken spirit dries up the bones.

Proverbs 17:22 NASB

Barbara Johnson says, "You have to look for the joy. Look for the light of God that is hitting your life, and you will find sparkles you didn't know were there."

Have you experienced that kind of joy? Hopefully so, because it's not enough to hear someone else talk about being joyful—you must actually experience that kind of joy in order to understand it.

Should you expect to be a joy-filled woman 24 hours a day, seven days a week, from this moment on? No. But you can (and should) experience pockets of joy frequently—that's the kind of joy-filled life that a woman like you deserves to live.

The Christian lifestyle is not one of legalistic do's and don'ts, but one that is positive, attractive, and joyful.

Vonette Bright

Finding joy means first of all finding Jesus.

Jill Briscoe

What is your focus today? Joy comes when it is Jesus first, others second . . . then you.

Kay Arthur

One Sunday a pastor told his congregation that the church needed some extra money, so he asked the people to prayerfully consider giving a little extra in the offering plate. He said that whoever gave the most cash would be able to pick out three hymns. After the offering plates were passed, the pastor glanced down and noticed that someone had placed a $1,000 bill in plate.

The pastor was so excited that he immediately shared his joy with the congregation and said he'd like to acknowledge the person who placed the money in the plate. So he asked who had given the money.

From the back of the sanctuary, a hand slowly went up—it was the spinster Miss Peabody. The pastor asked her to come down front, and slowly she made her way to the pastor. He told her how wonderful it was that she gave so much and he asked her to pick out three hymns.

The old lady's eyes brightened as she looked over the congregation, pointed to the three most handsome men in the building, and said, "I'll take him, and him, and him!"

Choosing to Be Kind

Our Father is kind; you be kind. "Don't pick on people, jump on their failures, criticize their faults— unless, of course, you want the same treatment. Don't condemn those who are down; that hardness can boomerang. Be easy on people; you'll find life a lot easier.

Luke 6:36-37 MSG

K indness is a choice. Sometimes, when we feel happy or generous, we find it easy to be kind. Other times, when we are discouraged or tired, we can scarcely summon the energy to utter a single kind word. But, God's commandment is clear: He intends that we make the conscious choice to treat others with kindness and respect, no matter our circumstances, no matter our emotions.

In the busyness and confusion of daily life, it is easy to lose focus, and it is easy to become frustrated. We are imperfect human beings struggling to manage our lives as best we can, but we often fall short. When we are distracted or disappointed, we may neglect to share a kind word or a kind deed. This oversight hurts others, but it hurts us most of all.

Today, slow yourself down and be alert for people who need your smile, your kind words, or your helping hand. Make kindness a centerpiece of your dealings with others. They will be blessed, and you will be too.

REAL INSIGHTS

Kindness in this world will do much to help others, not only to come into the light, but also to grow in grace day by day.

Fanny Crosby

Sometimes one little spark of kindness is all it takes to reignite the light of hope in a heart that's blinded by pain.

Barbara Johnson

One cold evening during the holiday season, a six-year-old boy was standing alone in front of a store window. The little child had ragged shoes, and his thin clothes were in tatters. A kind man noticed the little boy and took the child by the hand into the store.

There, he bought the youngster new shoes, a warm coat, pants, and a complete set of warm clothing.

As they walked back outside, the man said to the child, "Now, I hope you can go home and have a very happy holiday."

The little boy looked up at him and asked, "Sir, are you God?"

The man smiled down at the boy and replied, "No, son, I'm just one of His children."

The boy thought for a moment and said, "I knew you had to be some relation."

Enthused About Life

Whatever you do, do it enthusiastically,
as something done for the Lord and not for men.

Colossians 3:23 HCSB

Are you "burning" with enthusiasm about your life, your friends, your family, and your future? If so, congratulations, and keep up the good work! But, if your spiritual batteries are running low, perhaps you're spending too much energy focusing on your losses and too little time planning for future victories.

Writer Sara Jordan has this simple (but effective) advice: "Every day give yourself a good mental shampoo."

So if you're feeling tired or troubled, or both, don't despair. Instead, take time to count your blessings as you focus on things positive. And while you're at it, seek strength from the Source that never fails. When you sincerely petition God, He will give you all the strength you need to live victoriously through Him.

Catch on fire with enthusiasm and people will come for miles to watch you burn.

John Wesley

Enthusiasm, like the flu, is contagious—we get it from one another.

Barbara Johnson

One of the great needs in the church today is for every Christian to become enthusiastic about his faith in Jesus Christ.

Billy Graham

A teenager was sitting on a park bench reading his Bible when an "enlightened" man came by.

The man asked the teenager what he was reading, and the teenager responded enthusiastically, "I'm reading about the miracle when God parted the Red Sea."

The man was unimpressed: "Don't you know that modern science has proved that the Red Sea was only ten inches deep at the time? It was no problem for the Israelites to wade across."

The teenager thought for a moment and then became ever more excited. "That's amazing!" he said. "God is even greater than I thought—what a miracle! God got rid of the whole Egyptian army with only ten inches of water!"

The Power of Perseverance

*I have fought the good fight, I have finished the race,
I have kept the faith.*

2 Timothy 4:7 HCSB

As you continue to search for purpose in everyday life, you'll encounter your fair share of roadblocks and stumbling blocks; these situations require courage, patience, and above all, perseverance. As an example of perfect perseverance, we Christians need look no further than our Savior, Jesus Christ.

Jesus finished what He began. Despite the torture He endured, despite the shame of the cross, Jesus was steadfast in His faithfulness to God. We, too, must remain faithful, especially during times of hardship.

Perhaps you are in a hurry for God to reveal His plans for your life. If so, be forewarned: God operates on His own timetable, not yours. Sometimes, God may answer your prayers with silence, and when He does, you must patiently persevere. In times of trouble, you must remain steadfast and trust in the merciful goodness of your Heavenly Father. Whatever your problem, He can handle it. Your job is to keep persevering until He does.

REAL INSIGHTS

Your life is not a boring stretch of highway. It's a straight line to heaven. And just look at the fields ripening along the way. Look at the tenacity and endurance. Look at the grains of righteousness. You'll have quite a crop at harvest… so don't give up!

Joni Eareckson Tada

Failure is one of life's most powerful teachers. How we handle our failures determines whether we're going to simply "get by" in life or "press on."

Beth Moore

When you fall and skin your knees and skin your heart, He'll pick you up.

Charles Stanley

BUMPER STICKERS

CAUTION! CHURCH DRIVER OF THIS
VEHICLE SUBJECT TO FITS OF PRAISE!

I WORK FOR A JEWISH CARPENTER.

I'M A FOOL FOR CHRIST—
WHO'S FOOL ARE YOU?

The Best Policy

The honest person will live in safety,
but the dishonest will be caught.

Proverbs 10:9 NCV

It has been said on many occasions and in many ways that honesty is the best policy. For believers, it is far more important to note that honesty is God's policy. And if we are to be servants worthy of our Savior, Jesus Christ, we must be honest and forthright in our communications with others.

Sometimes, honesty is difficult; sometimes, honesty is painful; always, honesty is God's commandment. In the Book of Exodus, God did not command, "Thou shalt not bear false witness when it is convenient." And He didn't say, "Thou shalt not bear false witness most of the time." God said, "Thou shalt not bear false witness against thy neighbor." Period.

Sometime soon, perhaps even today, you will be tempted to bend the truth or perhaps even to break it. Resist that temptation. Truth is God's way . . . and it must also be yours. Period.

REAL INSIGHTS

The single most important element in any human relationship is honesty—with oneself, with God, and with others.

Catherine Marshall

Much guilt arises in the life of the believer from practicing the chameleon life of environmental adaptation.

Beth Moore

Integrity is not a given factor in everyone's life. It is a result of self-discipline, inner trust, and a decision to be relentlessly honest in all situations in our lives.

John Maxwell

Dear Priscilla,

I have been unable to sleep since I broke off our engagement. What a fool I was to end it. Won't you forgive and forget? Your absence is breaking my heart. I was an idiot—nobody will ever take your place. I love you with all my heart.

All my love,
John
xxxoooxxx

P.S. Congratulations on winning this week's lottery.

Taking Time to Say "Thanks"

Give thanks to the Lord, for He is good;
His faithful love endures forever.

Psalm 118:29 HCSB

If you're like most females on the planet, you're busy. Your life is probably hectic, demanding, and complicated. When the demands of life leave you rushing from place to place with scarcely a moment to spare, you may fail to pause and thank your Creator for the blessings He has bestowed upon you. Big mistake.

No matter how busy you are, you should never be too busy to thank God for His gifts. Your task, as an extreme follower of the living Christ, is to praise God many times each day. Then, with gratitude in your heart, you can face your daily duties with the perspective and power that only He can provide.

When you slow down and express your gratitude to your Heavenly Father, you enrich your own life and the lives of those around you. That's why thanksgiving should become a habit, a regular part of your daily routine. Yes, God has blessed you beyond measure, and you owe Him everything, including your eternal praise.

It is always possible to be thankful for what is given rather than to complain about what is not given. One or the other becomes a habit of life.

Elisabeth Elliot

Do you know that if at birth I had been able to make one petition, it would have been that I should be born blind? Because, when I get to heaven, the first face that shall ever gladden my sight will be that of my Savior!

Fanny Crosby

COMING SOON TO A CHURCH SIGN NEAR YOU...

IF YOU DON'T HAVE ANYTHING
TO PRAY ABOUT,
THANK GOD YOU DON'T.

DON'T HAVE ANYTHING TO BE
THANKFUL FOR?
CHECK YOUR PULSE!

IF YOU PAUSE TO THINK—
YOU'LL HAVE CAUSE TO THANK!

The Wisdom Not to Judge

Do not judge, or you too will be judged.
For in the same way you judge others, you will be judged,
and with the measure you use, it will be measured to you.

Matthew 7:1 NIV

Would you like a surefire formula for being unhappy? Here it is: spend as much time as you can judging other people. But if you'd rather be happy, remember this: in matters of judgment, God does not need (or want) your help. Why? Because God is perfectly capable of judging the human heart . . . while you are not. This message was made clear by the teachings of Jesus.

As Jesus came upon a young woman who had been condemned by the Pharisees, He spoke not only to the crowd that was gathered there, but also to all generations, when He warned, "He that is without sin among you, let him first cast a stone at her" (John 8:7 KJV).

Christ's message is straightforward: because we are all sinners, we are commanded to refrain from judging others. Yet the irony is this: it is precisely because we are sinners that we are so quick to judge.

All of us have fallen short of God's laws, and none of us, therefore, are qualified to "cast the first stone." Thankfully, God has forgiven us, and we, too, must forgive others. Let us refrain, then, from judging others. Instead, let us forgive them and love them in the same way that God has forgiven us.

A couple had two little boys, ages 8 and 10, who were excessively mischievous. They were always getting into trouble and their parents knew that if any mischief occurred in their town their sons were probably involved.

The boys' mother heard that a clergyman in town had been successful in disciplining children, so she asked if he would speak with her boys. The clergyman agreed, but asked to see them individually. So the mother sent her 8-year-old first, in the morning, with the older boy to see the clergyman in the afternoon.

The clergyman, a huge man with a booming voice, sat the younger boy down and asked him sternly, "Where is God?"

The boy's mouth dropped open, but he made no response. So the clergyman repeated the question in an even sterner tone, "Where is God!?" Again the boy made no attempt to answer. So the clergyman raised his voice even more and shook his finger in the boy's face and bellowed, "WHERE IS GOD!!!?"

The boy screamed and bolted from the room, ran directly home, and dove into his closet, slamming the door behind him. When his older brother found him in the closet, he asked, "What happened?"

The younger brother, gasping for breath, replied, "We are in BIG trouble this time, dude. God is missing—and they think WE did it!"

The Right Crowd

Greater love has no one than this,
that he lay down his life for his friends.

John 15:13 NIV

Do you want to be happy? Then make sure that you pick out friends who are happy, too. Why? Because happiness, like all human emotions, is contagious. When you associate with positive people, you'll feel better about yourself and your world—but when you hang around with negative people, you won't. So if you really want to feel better about yourself and your circumstances, you'll need to think carefully about the friends you choose to make—and the ones you choose to keep.

If you're really serious about being an optimistic, upbeat, hope-filled person, make sure that your friends feel the same way. Because if you become involved with upbeat people, you'll tend to be an upbeat person, too. But if you hang out with the critics, the cynics, and the naysayers, you'll find yourself becoming a cynic, too. And life is far too short for that.

The best times in life are made a thousand times better when shared with a dear friend.

Luci Swindoll

We long to find someone who has been where we've been, who shares our fragile skies, who sees our sunsets with the same shades of blue.

Beth Moore

A state trooper saw a car on the highway going 24 miles an hour, so he pulled the car over to make sure everything was all right. When he approached the driver, the trooper discovered she was a nun. "Excuse me, sister. But are you alright?" he asked. She replied, "Oh, yes, officer. We're just fine. Was I doing something wrong?" The officer said, "Well, sister, you were traveling way under the speed limit and I was concerned that you might be having car trouble or something." "But officer," the nun interrupted, "I saw a sign there about a mile back that said 24, and I know I wasn't going any faster than that."

Chuckling, the trooper said, "Sister, that was a state highway route marker; this is State Route 24, not the speed limit. The speed limit signs have MPH at the bottom." "Oh, now don't I feel foolish!" replied the nun.

About that time, the officer noticed three more nuns in the back seat; these three were quite pale and trembling violently. "Sister, what is wrong with your friends? Can I escort you to a hospital?" asked the trooper. "Oh, no, they're all right," she replied "We just turned off of Route 135."

Healthy Habits

Do not be deceived: "Evil company corrupts good habits."

1 Corinthians 15:33 NKJV

I t's an old saying and a true one: First, you make your habits, and then your habits make you. Some habits will inevitably bring you closer to God; other habits will lead you away from the path He has chosen for you. If you sincerely desire to improve your spiritual health, you must honestly examine the habits that make up the fabric of your day. And you must abandon those habits that are displeasing to God.

If you trust God, and if you keep asking for His help, He can transform your life. If you sincerely ask Him to help you, the same God who created the universe will help you defeat the harmful habits that have heretofore defeated you. So, if at first you don't succeed, keep praying. God is listening, and He's ready to help you become a better person if you ask Him . . . so ask today.

REAL INSIGHT

Prayer is a habit. Worship is a habit. Kindness is a habit. And if you want to please God, you'd better make sure that these habits are your habits.

Marie T. Freeman

You will never change your life until you change something you do daily.

John Maxwell

Since behaviors become habits, make them work with you and not against you.

E. Stanley Jones

COMING SOON TO A CHURCH SIGN NEAR YOU ...

GOD ANSWERS KNEE-MAIL.

JESUS:
NO LONG DISTANCE;
NO ROAMING CHARGES;
ALWAYS AN OPEN LINE.

Imitating Christ

Therefore, be imitators of God, as dearly loved children.

Ephesians 5:1 HCSB

Imitating Christ is impossible, but attempting to imitate Him is both possible and advisable. By attempting to imitate Jesus, we seek, to the best of our abilities, to walk in His footsteps. To the extent we succeed in following Him, we receive the spiritual abundance that is the rightful possession of those who love Christ and keep His commandments.

Do you seek God's blessings for the day ahead? Then, to the best of your abilities, imitate His Son. You will fall short, of course. But if your heart is right and your intentions are pure, God will bless your efforts, your day, and your life.

You cannot cooperate with Jesus in becoming what He wants you to become and simultaneously be what the world desires to make you. If you would say, "Take the world but give me Jesus," then you must deny yourself and take up your cross. The simple truth is that your "self" must be put to death in order for you to get to the point where for you to live is Christ. What will it be? The world and you, or Jesus and you? You do have a choice to make.

Kay Arthur

REAL INSIGHTS

Every Christian is to become a little Christ. The whole purpose of becoming a Christian is simply nothing else.

C. S. Lewis

A person who gazes and keeps on gazing at Jesus becomes like him in appearance.

E. Stanley Jones

Christlikeness is not produced by imitation, but by inhabitation.

Rick Warren

COMING SOON TO A CHURCH SIGN NEAR YOU ...

IF YOU WERE ON TRIAL FOR BEING
A CHRISTIAN,
WOULD THERE BE ENOUGH
EVIDENCE TO CONVICT YOU?

CHRISTIANS ARE LIKE COALS OF A FIRE.
TOGETHER THEY GLOW—
APART THEY GROW COLD.

CHRISTIANS, LIKE PIANOS,
NEED FREQUENT TUNING!

So Laugh!

There is a time for everything, and everything on earth has its special season . . . . There is a time to cry and a time to laugh. There is a time to be sad and a time to dance.

Ecclesiastes 3:1,4 NCV

Laughter is a gift from God, a gift that He intends for us to use. Yet sometimes, because of the inevitable stresses of everyday living, we fail to find the fun in life. When we allow life's inevitable disappointments to cast a pall over our lives and our souls, we do a profound disservice to ourselves and to our loved ones.

If you've allowed the clouds of life to obscure the blessings of life, perhaps you've formed the unfortunate habit of taking things just a little too seriously. If so, it's time to fret a little less and laugh a little more.

So today, look for the humor that most certainly surrounds you—when you do, you'll find it. And remember: God created laughter for a reason . . . and Father indeed knows best. So laugh!

REAL INSIGHTS

As you're rushing through life, take time to stop a moment, look into people's eyes, say something kind, and try to make them laugh!

Barbara Johnson

He who laughs lasts—he who doesn't, doesn't.

Marie T. Freeman

I want to encourage you in these days with your family to lighten up and enjoy. Laugh a little bit; it might just set you free.

Dennis Swanberg

COMING SOON TO A CHURCH SIGN NEAR YOU...

LAUGH UNTIL YOU FEEL BETTER—
AND THE DEVIL FEELS WORSE!

LAUGHTER IS LIKE PREMIUM GASOLINE:
IT TAKES THE KNOCK OUT OF LIVING.

SHINE—DON'T WHINE.

Quiet Time with God

Knowing God leads to self-control. Self-control leads to patient endurance, and patient endurance leads to godliness.

2 Peter 1:6 NLT

Do you ever wonder if God is really "right here, right now"? Do you wonder if God hears your prayers, if He understands your feelings, or if He really knows your heart? If so, you're not alone: lots of very faithful Christians have experienced periods of doubt. In fact, some of the biggest heroes in the Bible had plenty of doubts—and so, perhaps, will you. But when you have doubts, remember this: God isn't on a coffee break, and He hasn't moved out of town. God isn't taking a long vacation, and He isn't snoozing on the couch. He's right here, right now, listening to your thoughts and prayers, watching over your every move.

The Bible teaches that a wonderful way to get to know God is simply to be still and listen to Him. But sometimes, you may find it hard to slow down and listen. As the demands of everyday life weigh down upon you, you may be tempted to ignore God's presence or—worse yet—to rebel against His commandments. But, when you quiet yourself and acknowledge His presence, God touches your heart and restores your spirits. So why not let Him do it right now? If you really want to know Him better, silence is a wonderful place to start.

REAL INSIGHTS

Knowing God involves an intimate, personal relationship that is developed over time through prayer and getting answers to prayer, through Bible study and applying its teaching to our lives, through obedience and experiencing the power of God, through moment-by-moment submission to Him that results in a moment-by-moment filling of the Holy Spirit.

Anne Graham Lotz

Here is our opportunity: we cannot see God, but we can see Christ. Christ was not only the Son of God, but He was the Father. Whatever Christ was, that God is.

Hannah Whitall Smith

SMILE!

A kindergarten teacher was observing her students while they drew pictures. As she came to one little boy who was working diligently, she asked what he was drawing.

The boy replied, "I'm drawing God."

The teacher paused and said, "But no one knows what God looks like."

Without missing a beat, the boy replied, "They will in a minute."

God's Timetable

He has made everything beautiful in its time.
He has also set eternity in the hearts of men;
yet they cannot fathom what God has done
from beginning to end.

Ecclesiastes 3:11 NIV

We should learn to trust God's timing, but we are sorely tempted to do otherwise. Why? Because we human beings are usually anxious for things to happen sooner rather than later. But, God knows better.

God has created a world that unfolds according to His own timetable, not ours . . . thank goodness! We mortals might make a terrible mess of things. God does not. God's plan does not always happen in the way that we would like or at the time of our own choosing. Our task is to wait patiently and never lose hope.

In the words of Elisabeth Elliot, "We must learn to move according to the timetable of the Timeless One, and to be at peace." That's advice worth following today, tomorrow, and every day of your life.

REAL INSIGHTS

When there is perplexity there is always guidance—not always at the moment we ask, but in good time, which is God's time. There is no need to fret and stew.

Elisabeth Elliot

Your times are in His hands. He's in charge of the timetable, so wait patiently.

Kay Arthur

He has the right to interrupt your life. He is Lord. When you accepted Him as Lord, you gave Him the right to help Himself to your life anytime He wants.

Henry Blackaby

COMING SOON TO A CHURCH SIGN NEAR YOU ...

DON'T PUT A QUESTION MARK
WHERE GOD PUT A PERIOD.

WHEN YOU ARE IN DEEP WATER—
TRUST THE ONE WHO WALKED ON IT.

JESUS.
DON'T LEAVE EARTH WITHOUT HIM!

Media Messages

Set your minds on what is above, not on what is on the earth.

Colossians 3:2 HCSB

Sometimes it's hard being a Christian, especially when the world keeps pumping out messages that are contrary to your faith.

The media is working around the clock in an attempt to rearrange your priorities. The media says that your appearance is all-important, that your clothes are all-important, that your possessions are all-important. But guess what? Those messages are lies. The "all-important" things in your life have little to do with possessions or appearances. The all-important things in life have to do with your faith, your family, and your future. Period.

Are you willing to stand up for your faith? Are you willing to stand up and be counted, not just in church, where it's relatively easy to be a Christian, but also out there in the "real" world, where it's hard? Hopefully so, because you owe it to God and you owe it to yourself.

As we have by faith said no to sin, so we should by faith say yes to God and set our minds on things above, where Christ is seated in the heavenlies.

Vonette Bright

The more we stuff ourselves with material pleasures, the less we seem to appreciate life.

Barbara Johnson

Our fight is not against any physical enemy; it is against organizations and powers that are spiritual. We must struggle against sin all our lives, but we are assured we will win.

Corrie ten Boom

The minister was preoccupied with thoughts of how he was going to ask the congregation to come up with more money than they were expecting for repairs to the church building. So, he was annoyed to find that the regular organist was sick and a substitute had been brought in at the last minute.

The substitute wanted to know what to play.

"Here's a copy of the service," he said impatiently. "But you'll have to think of something to play after I make the announcement about the finances."

During the service, the minister paused and said, "Brothers and Sisters, we are in great difficulty; the roof repairs cost twice as much as we expected, and we need $4,000 more. Any of you who can pledge $100 or more, please stand up."

At that moment, the substitute organist played the National Anthem . . . and that's how the substitute organist became the permanent organist!

Making Time to Praise God

Therefore, through Him let us continually offer up
to God a sacrifice of praise, that is,
the fruit of our lips that confess His name.

Hebrews 13:15 HCSB

Your life is probably hectic, demanding, and complicated. And when the demands of life leave you rushing from place to place with scarcely a moment to spare, you may not take time to praise your Creator. Big mistake.

The Bible makes it clear: it pays to praise God. Worship and praise should be a part of everything you do. Otherwise, you quickly lose perspective as you fall prey to the demands of everyday life.

Do you sincerely desire to know God in a more meaningful way? Then praise Him for who He is and for what He has done for you. And please don't wait until Sunday morning—praise Him all day long, every day, for as long as you live . . . and then for all eternity.

Two wings are necessary to lift our souls toward God: prayer and praise. Prayer asks. Praise accepts the answer.

Mrs. Charles E. Cowman

Nothing we do is more powerful or more life-changing than praising God.

Stormie Omartian

An elderly lady was well known for her faith, and for her boldness in talking about it. She would often stand on her front porch and shout, "PRAISE THE LORD!"

Next door to the woman lived an atheist who would become so angry at her proclamations that he would shout, "There ain't no Lord!"

Hard times set in upon the old lady, so she prayed to God for assistance. She stood on her porch and shouted, "PRAISE THE LORD, I'M HAVING A HARD TIME. I NEED FOOD. PLEASE, LORD, SEND ME SOME GROCERIES!!"

The next morning, when the lady went out on her front porch, she looked down and found a big bag of groceries. She shouted, "PRAISE THE LORD!" But at that moment, her atheist neighbor jumped from behind a bush and screamed, "Aha! I told you there was no Lord. I bought those groceries; God didn't."

The old lady became even more excited. "PRAISE THE LORD," she cried. "GOD DIDN'T JUST SEND ME GROCERIES! HE EVEN GOT THE DEVIL TO PAY FOR 'EM! PRAISE THE LORD!"

Every Day with God

Stay clear of silly stories that get dressed up as religion.
Exercise daily in God—no spiritual flabbiness, please!

1 Timothy 4:7 MSG

Want to know God better? Then schedule a meeting with Him every day.

Daily life is a tapestry of habits, and no habit is more important to your spiritual health than the discipline of daily prayer and devotion to the Creator. When you begin each day with your head bowed and your heart lifted, you are reminded of God's love and God's laws.

Each day has 1,440 minutes—do you value your relationship with God enough to spend a few of those minutes with Him? He deserves that much of your time and more. But if you find that you're simply "too busy" for a daily chat with your Father in heaven, it's time to take a long, hard look at your priorities and your values.

If you've acquired the unfortunate habit of trying to "squeeze" God into the corners of your life, it's time to reshuffle the items on your to-do list by placing God first. God wants your undivided attention, not the leftovers of your day. So, if you haven't already done so, form the habit of spending quality time with your Creator. He deserves it . . . and so, for that matter, do you.

FAVORITE HYMNS BY PROFESSION

The Dentist's Hymn: Crown Him with Many Crowns

The Tailor's Hymn: Holy, Holy, Holy

The Golfer's Hymn: There Is a Green Hill Far Away

The Politician's Hymn: Standing on the Promises

The Optometrist's Hymn: Open My Eyes That I May See

The IRS Agent's Hymn: I Surrender All

The Gossip's Hymn: Pass It On

The Electrician's Hymn: Send the Light

The Shopper's Hymn: In the Sweet By and By

The Pilot's Hymn: I'll Fly Away

The Judge's Hymn: Almost Persuaded

The Baker's Hymn: When the Roll Is Called Up Yonder

The Shoe Repairer's Hymn: It Is Well with My Soul

He Answers

And everything—whatever you ask in prayer,
believing—you will receive.

Matthew 21:22 HCSB

I n case you've been wondering, wonder no more—God does answer your prayers. What God does not do is this: He does not always answer your prayers as soon as you might like, and He does not always answer your prayers by saying "Yes."

God isn't an order-taker, and He's not some sort of cosmic vending machine. Sometimes—even when we want something very badly—our loving Heavenly Father responds to our requests by saying "No," and we must accept His answer, even if we don't understand it.

God answers prayers not only according to our wishes but also according to His master plan. We cannot know that plan, but we can know the Planner . . . and we must trust His wisdom, His righteousness, and His love.

Of this you can be sure: God is listening, and He wants to hear from you now. So what are you waiting for?

REAL INSIGHTS

As we join together in prayer, we draw on God's enabling might in a way that multiplies our own efforts many times over.

Shirley Dobson

When you ask God to do something, don't ask timidly; put your whole heart into it.

Marie T. Freeman

When there is a matter that requires definite prayer, pray until you believe God and until you can thank Him for His answer.

Hannah Whitall Smith

The Wednesday-night church service coincided with the last day of hunting season. The pastor asked who had bagged a deer. No one raised a hand.

Puzzled, the pastor said, "I don't understand. Last Sunday many of you said you were missing because of hunting season. I had the whole congregation pray for your deer."

One hunter groaned, "Well, it worked. They're all safe."

The Best Time to Celebrate

Celebrate God all day, every day. I mean, revel in him!

Philippians 4:4 MSG

What is the best day to celebrate life? This one! Today and every day should be a time for celebration as we consider the Good News of God's gift: salvation through Jesus Christ.

What do you expect from the day ahead? Are you expecting God to do wonderful things, or are you living beneath a cloud of worry and doubt?

The familiar words of Psalm 118:24 remind us of a profound yet simple truth: "This is the day which the LORD has made." Our duty, as believers, is to rejoice in God's marvelous creation. For Christians, every day begins and ends with God and His Son. Christ came to this earth to give us abundant life and eternal salvation. We give thanks to our Maker when we treasure each day. So with no further ado, let the celebration begin!

Our sense of joy, satisfaction, and fulfillment in life increases, no matter what the circumstances, if we are in the center of God's will.

Billy Graham

BIBLE CHARACTERS AND THEIR FAVORITE SONGS:

Noah: "Raindrops Keep Falling on My Head"

Adam and Eve: "Strangers in Paradise"

Moses: "The Wanderer"

Lazarus: "The Second Time Around"

Samson: "Hair"

Job: "I've Got a Right to Sing the Blues"

Daniel: "The Lion Sleeps Tonight"

Jezebel: "The Lady Is a Tramp"

Shadrach, Meshach, and Abednego: "Great Balls of Fire!"

Joshua: "Good Vibrations"

Peter: "I'm Sorry"

The Three Kings: "When You Wish Upon a Star"

Elijah: "Up, Up, and Away"

Methuselah: "Stayin' Alive"

You'd Better Beware

The Lord is pleased with a good person,
but he will punish anyone who plans evil.

Proverbs 12:2 NCV

Face facts: this world is inhabited by quite a few people who are very determined to do evil things. The devil and his human helpers are working 24/7 to cause pain and heartbreak in every corner of the globe . . . including your corner. So you'd better beware.

Your job, if you choose to accept it, is to recognize evil and fight it. The moment that you decide to fight evil whenever you see it, you can no longer be a lukewarm, halfhearted Christian. And, when you are no longer a lukewarm Christian, God rejoices while the devil despairs.

When will you choose to get serious about fighting the evils of our world? Before you answer that question, consider this: in the battle of good versus evil, the devil never takes a day off . . . and neither should you.

REAL INSIGHTS

Light is stronger than darkness—darkness cannot "comprehend" or "overcome" it.

Anne Graham Lotz

Where God's ministers are most successful, there the powers of darkness marshal their forces for the conflict.

Lottie Moon

We are in a continual battle with the spiritual forces of evil, but we will triumph when we yield to God's leading and call on His powerful presence in prayer.

Shirley Dobson

SMILE!

A child was watching his mother delete a long list of junk E-mail on the computer screen.

"This reminds me of the Lord's Prayer," the child said.

"What do you mean?" the mother asked.

"You know," the child replied, "the part about 'deliver us from E-mail.'"

Peer Pressure 101

We must obey God rather than men.

Acts 5:29 HCSB

Okay, girlfriend, here's an important question: Are you a people-pleaser or a God-pleaser? Hopefully, you're far more concerned with pleasing God than you are with pleasing people. But face facts: even if you're a devoted Christian, you're still going to feel the urge to impress your friends and acquaintances—and sometimes that urge will be strong.

Peer pressure can be good or bad, depending upon who your peers are and how they behave. If your friends encourage you to follow God's will and to obey His commandments, then you'll experience positive peer pressure, and that's a good thing. But, if your friends encourage you to do foolish things, then you're facing a different kind of peer pressure . . . and you'd better beware. When you feel pressured to do things—or to say things—that lead you away from God, you're heading straight for trouble. So don't do the "easy" thing or the "popular" thing. Do the right thing, and don't worry about winning any popularity contests.

Are you satisfied to follow the crowd? If so, you will probably pay a heavy price for your shortsightedness. But if you're determined to follow the One from Galilee, He will guide your steps and bless your undertakings. To sum it up, here's your choice: you can choose to please God first, or you can fall victim to peer pressure. The choice is yours—and so are the consequences.

REAL INSIGHTS

We, as God's people, are not only to stay far away from sin and sinners who would entice us, but we are to be so like our God that we mourn over sin.

Kay Arthur

You will get untold flak for prioritizing God's revealed and present will for your life over man's . . . but, boy, is it worth it.

Beth Moore

COMING SOON TO A CHURCH SIGN NEAR YOU . . .

A PERSON WHO HUNGERS FOR
THE WORLD'S APPROVAL
WILL STARVE TO DEATH SPIRITUALLY!

IF AT FIRST YOU DON'T SUCCEED,
READ THE INSTRUCTION MANUAL—GOD'S.

GET RICH QUICK!
COUNT YOUR BLESSINGS!

You and Your Family

Unless the Lord builds a house,
its builders labor over it in vain; unless the Lord
watches over a city, the watchman stays alert in vain.

Psalm 127:1 HCSB

As every woman knows, family life is a mixture of conversations, mediations, irritations, deliberations, commiserations, frustrations, negotiations and celebrations. In other words, the life of the typical mom is incredibly varied.

Certainly, in the life of every family, there are moments of frustration and disappointment. Lots of them. But, for those who are lucky enough to live in the presence of a close-knit, caring clan, the rewards far outweigh the frustrations. That's why we pray fervently for our family members, and that's why we love them despite their faults.

No family is perfect, and neither is yours. But, despite the inevitable challenges and occasional hurt feelings of family life, your clan is God's gift to you. That little band of men, women, kids, and babies is a priceless treasure on temporary loan from the Father above. Give thanks to the Giver for the gift of family . . . and act accordingly.

REAL INSIGHTS

For whatever life holds for you and your family in the coming days, weave the unfailing fabric of God's Word through your heart and mind. It will hold strong, even if the rest of life unravels.

Gigi Graham Tchividjian

One way or the other, God, who thought up the family in the first place, has the very best idea of how to bring sense to the chaos of broken relationships we see all around us. I really believe that if I remain still and listen a lot, He will share some solutions with me so I can share them with others.

Jill Briscoe

SMILE!

A little girl was attending her first wedding. After the service, her cousin asked her, "How many women can a man marry?"

"Sixteen," the girl responded.

Her cousin was amazed that she had an answer so quickly. "How do you know that?"

"Easy," the little girl said. "All you have to do is add it up, like the pastor said: 4 better, 4 worse, 4 richer, 4 poorer."

Fully Grown?

Grow in grace and understanding of our Master and Savior, Jesus Christ. Glory to the Master, now and forever! Yes!

2 Peter 3:18 MSG

Are you a fully-grown woman? Physically yes. But spiritually? No way! And thank goodness that you're not! Even if you're a very mature person—even if you're a righteous, spiritual, godly woman—you've still got lots of room to grow.

The 19th-century writer Hannah Whitall Smith observed, "The maturity of a Christian experience cannot be reached in a moment." No kidding. In truth, the search for spiritual growth lasts a lifetime.

When we cease to grow, either emotionally or spiritually, we do ourselves and our families a profound disservice. But, if we study God's Word, if we obey His commandments, and if we live in the center of His will, we will not be "stagnant" believers; we will, instead, be growing Christians . . . and that's exactly what God wants for our lives. Come to think of it, that's exactly what you should want, too.

There is wonderful freedom and joy in coming to recognize that the fun is in the becoming.

Gloria Gaither

Our heavenly Father knows to place us where we may learn lessons impossible anywhere else. He has neither misplaced nor displaced us.

Elisabeth Elliot

Kindness in this world will do much to help others, not only to come into the light, but also to grow in grace day by day.

Fanny Crosby

A man was stranded on a deserted island, and many years passed before he was finally discovered. When the rescue party came ashore, the man expressed his gratitude and told them how he had survived alone for so many years. But the rescue party was suspicious because they believed that nobody could survive on an island alone for so long. "But it's true," the man said, "Come and see where I lived."

When the rescue party arrived at the man's home, they saw three huts. "Ah hah!" they said. "There are three huts here, which proves you were not alone."

"No," said the man, "let me explain. This first hut is where I lived all those years, and the third hut is where I attended church."

"What, then, is the second hut?" they inquired.

"Oh," said the man, "that's where I used to go to church."

Controlling Your Temper

My dear brothers and sisters, be quick to listen,
slow to speak, and slow to get angry.
Your anger can never make things right in God's sight.

James 1:19-20 NLT

Your temper is either your master or your servant. Either you control it, or it controls you. And the extent to which you allow anger to rule your life will determine, to a surprising degree, the quality of your relationships with others and your relationship with God.

Temper tantrums are usually unproductive, unattractive, unforgettable, and unnecessary. Perhaps that's why Proverbs 16:32 states that, "Controlling your temper is better than capturing a city" (NCV).

If you've allowed anger to become a regular visitor at your house, you should pray for wisdom, for patience, and for a heart that is so filled with forgiveness that it contains no room for bitterness. God will help you terminate your tantrums if you ask Him to—and that's a good thing because anger and peace cannot coexist in the same mind.

REAL INSIGHTS

Life is too short to spend it being angry, bored, or dull.

Barbara Johnson

Anger unresolved will only bring you woe.

Kay Arthur

Anger is the noise of the soul; the unseen irritant of the heart; the relentless invader of silence.

Max Lucado

COMING SOON TO A CHURCH SIGN NEAR YOU ...

WHEN YOU GET HOT UNDER THE COLLAR,
MAKE SURE YOUR HEART IS
PRAYER-CONDITIONED.

IS THERE SOMEBODY WHO'S
ALWAYS GETTING YOUR GOAT?
TALK TO THE SHEPHERD.

YOU DON'T HAVE TO ATTEND
EVERY ARGUMENT YOU'RE INVITED TO!

Considering the Cross

But as for me, I will never boast about anything except the cross of our Lord Jesus Christ, through whom the world has been crucified to me, and I to the world.

Galatians 6:14 HCSB

As we consider Christ's sacrifice on the cross, we should be profoundly humbled and profoundly grateful. And today, as we come to Christ in prayer, we should do so in a spirit of quiet, heartfelt devotion to the One who gave His life so that we might have life eternal.

He was the Son of God, but He wore a crown of thorns. He was the Savior of mankind, yet He was put to death on a rough hewn cross made of wood. He offered His healing touch to an unsaved world, and yet the same hands that had healed the sick and raised the dead were pierced with nails.

Christ humbled Himself on a cross—for you. He shed His blood—for you. He has offered to walk with you through this life and throughout all eternity. As you approach Him today in prayer, think about His sacrifice and His grace. And be humble.

REAL INSIGHTS

God is my heavenly Father. He loves me with an everlasting love. The proof of that is the Cross.

Elisabeth Elliot

The cross takes care of the past. The cross takes care of the flesh. The cross takes care of the world.

Kay Arthur

Jesus challenges you and me to keep our focus daily on the cross of His will if we want to be His disciples.

Anne Graham Lotz

COMING SOON TO A CHURCH SIGN NEAR YOU ...

NAILS DIDN'T HOLD JESUS ON THE CROSS.
HIS LOVE FOR YOU DID.

THE CROSS IS GOD'S WAY OF MAKING
A PLUS SIGN OUT OF A MINUS.

THE CROSS IS GOD'S COMPASS
POINTING TO HEAVEN.

The Gift of Eternal Life

For God so loved the world that he gave his only Son,
so that everyone who believes in him will not perish
but have eternal life.

John 3:16 NLT

Eternal life is not an event that begins when you die. Eternal life begins when you invite Jesus into your heart right here on earth. So it's important to remember that God's plans for you are not limited to the ups and downs of everyday life. If you've allowed Jesus to reign over your heart, you've already begun your eternal journey.

As mere mortals, our vision for the future, like our lives here on earth, is limited. God's vision is not burdened by such limitations: His plans extend throughout all eternity.

Let us praise the Creator for His priceless gift, and let us share the Good News with all who cross our paths. We return our Father's love by accepting His grace and by sharing His message and His love. When we do, we are blessed here on earth and throughout all eternity.

The gift of God is eternal life, spiritual life, abundant life through faith in Jesus Christ, the Living Word of God.

Anne Graham Lotz

REAL INSIGHT

I can still hardly believe it. I, with shriveled, bent fingers, atrophied muscles, gnarled knees, and no feeling from the shoulders down, will one day have a new body—light, bright and clothed in righteousness—powerful and dazzling.

Joni Eareckson Tada

A sick woman turned to her doctor, as she was leaving the room after paying a visit, and said, "Doctor, I am afraid to die. Tell me what lies on the other side." Very quietly the doctor said, "I don't know." "You don't know? You, a Christian man, do not know what is on the other side?" The doctor was holding the handle of the door, on the other side of which came a sound of scratching and whining, and as he opened the door a dog sprang into the room and leaped on him with an eager show of gladness.

Turning to the patient, the doctor said, "Did you notice my dog? He's never been in this room before. He didn't know what was inside. He knew nothing except that his master was here, and when the door opened he sprang in without fear. I know little of what is on the other side of death, but I do know one thing: I know my Master is there, and that is enough. And when the door opens, I shall pass through with no fear, but with gladness."

Forgiveness Now

Be gentle with one another, sensitive.
Forgive one another as quickly and thoroughly
as God in Christ forgave you.

Ephesians 4:32 MSG

Are you the kind of woman who has a tough time forgiving and forgetting? If so, welcome to the club. Most of us find it difficult to forgive the people who have hurt us. And that's too bad because life would be much simpler if we could forgive people "once and for all" and be done with it. Yet forgiveness is seldom that easy. Usually, the decision to forgive is straightforward, but the process of forgiving is more difficult. Forgiveness is a journey that requires effort, time, perseverance, and prayer.

If there exists even one person whom you have not forgiven (and that includes yourself), obey God's commandment: forgive that person today. And remember that bitterness, anger, and regret are not part of God's plan for your life. Forgiveness is.

If you sincerely wish to forgive someone, pray for that person. And then pray for yourself by asking God to heal your heart. Don't expect forgiveness to be easy or quick, but rest assured: with God as your partner, you can forgive . . . and you will.

REAL INSIGHTS

God expects us to forgive others as He has forgiven us; we are to follow His example by having a forgiving heart.

Vonette Bright

I believe that forgiveness can become a continuing cycle: because God forgives us, we're to forgive others; because we forgive others, God forgives us. Scripture presents both parts of the cycle.

Shirley Dobson

COMING SOON TO A CHURCH SIGN NEAR YOU ...

TGIF—THANK GOD I'M FORGIVEN.

WHEN YOU HARBOR BITTERNESS,
HAPPINESS WILL DOCK ELSEWHERE.

AN EYE FOR AN EYE
AND A TOOTH FOR A TOOTH ...
AND PRETTY SOON,
EVERYBODY'S BLIND
AND WEARING DENTURES.

Fitness Matters

Whatever you eat or drink or whatever you do,
you must do all for the glory of God.

1 Corinthians 10:31 NLT

Are you shaping up or spreading out? Do you eat sensibly and exercise regularly, or do you spend most of your time on the couch with a Twinkie in one hand and a clicker in the other? Are you choosing to treat your body like a temple or a trash heap? How you answer these questions will help determine how long you live and how well you live.

Physical fitness is a choice, a choice that requires discipline—it's as simple as that. But here's the catch: understanding the need for discipline is easy, but leading a disciplined life can be hard. Why? Because it's usually more fun to eat a second piece of cake than it is to jog a second lap around the track. But, as we survey the second helpings that all too often find their way on to our plates, we should consider this: as Christians, we are instructed to lead disciplined lives, and when we behave in undisciplined ways, we are living outside God's will.

We live in a world in which leisure is glorified and consumption is commercialized. But God has other plans. He did not create us for lives of gluttony or laziness; He created us for far greater things.

God has a plan for every aspect of your life, and His plan includes provisions for your physical health. But, He expects you to do your fair share of the work! In a world that is chock-full of tasty temptations, you may find it all too easy to make unhealthy choices. Your challenge, of course, is to resist those unhealthy temptations by every means you can, including prayer. And rest assured: when you ask for God's help, He will give it.

A fundamentalist Christian couple felt it was important to own an equally fundamentalist Christian pet. So, they went shopping. At a kennel specializing in this particular breed, they found a dog they liked. When they asked the dog to fetch the Bible, Fido did it in a flash. When they instructed him to look up Psalm 23, Fido complied, using his paws with dexterity. So the couple purchased the animal and went home.

That night, the couple had friends over. They were so proud of their new fundamentalist dog and his major skills that they called the dog over and put him through his paces. The friends were impressed, of course, but they also wondered if the dog could do any of the usual dog tricks as well. This question stopped the couple cold, as they hadn't thought about any normal pet tricks.

"Well," they said, "let's try this out." Once more they called out to the dog and then clearly pronounced the command, "Heel!" Quick as a wink, the dog jumped up, put his paw on the man's forehead, closed his eyes in concentration, and bowed his head.

Patience NOW!

A patient person [shows] great understanding,
but a quick-tempered one promotes foolishness.

Proverbs 14:29 HCSB

Are you a woman in a hurry? If so, you may be in for a few disappointments. Why? Because life has a way of unfolding according to God's timetable, not yours. That's why life requires patience . . . and lots of it!

Lamentations 3:25-26 reminds us that, "The Lord is wonderfully good to those who wait for him and seek him. So it is good to wait quietly for salvation from the Lord" (NIV). But, for most of us, waiting quietly for God is difficult because we're in such a hurry for things to happen!

The next time you find your patience tested to the limit, slow down and trust God. Sometimes, we must wait patiently for Him, and that's as it should be. After all, think how patient God has been with us.

Let me encourage you to continue to wait with faith. God may not perform a miracle, but He is trustworthy to touch you and make you whole where there used to be a hole.

Lisa Whelchel

REAL INSIGHTS

If you want to hear God's voice clearly and you are uncertain, then remain in His presence until He changes that uncertainty. Often much can happen during this waiting for the Lord. Sometimes he changes pride into humility; doubt into faith and peace . . . .

Corrie ten Boom

He makes us wait. He keeps us in the dark on purpose. He makes us walk when we want to run, sit still when we want to walk, for he has things to do in our souls that we are not interested in.

Elisabeth Elliot

COMING SOON TO A CHURCH SIGN NEAR YOU . . .

PATIENCE IS A VIRTUE
THAT CARRIES A LOT OF WAIT.

GOD MAY SAY "WAIT,"
BUT HE NEVER SAYS, "WORRY."

GOD GAVE EVERYONE PATIENCE—
WISE PEOPLE USE IT.

When You Have Doubts

Now if any of you lacks wisdom, he should ask God, who gives to all generously and without criticizing, and it will be given to him. But let him ask in faith without doubting. For the doubter is like the surging sea, driven and tossed by the wind.

James 1:5-6 HCSB

If you've never had any doubts about your faith, then you can stop reading this page now and skip to the next. But if you've ever been plagued by doubts about your faith or your God, keep reading.

Even some of the most faithful Christians are, at times, beset by occasional bouts of discouragement and doubt. But even when we feel far removed from God, God is never far removed from us. He is always with us, always willing to calm the storms of life—always willing to replace our doubts with comfort and assurance.

Whenever you're plagued by doubts, that's precisely the moment you should seek God's presence by genuinely seeking to establish a deeper, more meaningful relationship with His Son. Then you may rest assured that in time, God will calm your fears, answer your prayers, and restore your confidence.

REAL INSIGHTS

We are most vulnerable to the piercing winds of doubt when we distance ourselves from the mission and fellowship to which Christ has called us.

Joni Eareckson Tada

Fear and doubt are conquered by a faith that rejoices. And faith can rejoice because the promises of God are as certain as God Himself.

Kay Arthur

Mark it down. God never turns away the honest seeker. Go to God with your questions. You may not find all the answers, but in finding God, you know the One who does.

Max Lucado

COMING SOON TO A CHURCH SIGN NEAR YOU ...

FEED YOUR FAITH, AND YOUR DOUBTS
WILL STARVE TO DEATH.

IF YOU FIND YOURSELF
WITH TIME ON YOUR HANDS—
PUT 'EM TOGETHER AND PRAY.

Time for Fun

So I recommend having fun, because there is nothing better for people to do in this world than to eat, drink, and enjoy life. That way they will experience some happiness along with all the hard work God gives them.

Ecclesiastes 8:15 NLT

Are you a woman who takes time each day to really enjoy life? Hopefully so. After all, you are the recipient of a precious gift—the gift of life. And because God has seen fit to give you this gift, it is incumbent upon you to use it and to enjoy it. But sometimes, amid the inevitable pressures of everyday living, really enjoying life may seem almost impossible. It is not.

For most of us, fun is as much a function of attitude as it is a function of environment. So whether you're standing victorious atop one of life's mountains or trudging through one of life's valleys, enjoy yourself. You deserve to have fun today, and God wants you to have fun today . . . so what on earth are you waiting for?

Our thoughts, not our circumstances, determine our happiness.

John Maxwell

REAL INSIGHTS

Whence comes this idea that if what we are doing is fun, it can't be God's will? The God who made giraffes, a baby's fingernails, a puppy's tail, a crooknecked squash, the bobwhite's call, and a young girl's giggle, has a sense of humor. Make no mistake about that.

Catherine Marshall

I became aware of one very important concept I had missed before: my attitude—not my circumstances—was what was making me unhappy.

Vonette Bright

A preacher was completing a temperance sermon. With great expression he said, "If I had all the beer in the world, I'd take it and throw it in the river."

With even greater emphasis he said, "And if I had all the wine in the world, I'd take it and throw it in the river."

And then finally, he said, "And if I had all the whiskey in the world, I'd take it and throw it in the river."

He sat down.

The song leader then stood up very cautiously and announced with a smile, "For our closing song, let us sing Hymn # 365: "Shall We Gather at the River."

Beyond Temptation

But remember that the temptations that come into your life are no different from what others experience. And God is faithful. He will keep the temptation from becoming so strong that you can't stand up against it. When you are tempted, he will show you a way out so that you will not give in to it.

1 Corinthians 10:13 NLT

Face facts: you live in a temptation-filled world. The devil is hard at work in your neighborhood, and so are his helpers. Here in the 21st century, the bad guys are working around the clock to lead you astray. That's why you must remain vigilant.

In a letter to believers, Peter offers a stern warning: "Your adversary, the devil, prowls around like a roaring lion, seeking someone to devour" (1 Peter 5:8 NASB). What was true in New Testament times is equally true in our own. Satan tempts his prey and then devours them (and it's up to you—and only you—to make sure that you're not one of the ones being devoured!).

As a believer who seeks a radical relationship with Jesus, you must beware because temptations are everywhere. Satan is determined to win; you must be equally determined that he does not.

REAL INSIGHTS

Do not fight the temptation in detail. Turn from it. Look ONLY at your Lord. Sing. Read. Work.

Amy Carmichael

Because Christ has faced our every temptation without sin, we never face a temptation that has no door of escape.

Beth Moore

Temptation is not a sin. Even Jesus was tempted. The Lord Jesus gives you the strength needed to resist temptation.

Corrie ten Boom

COMING SOON TO A CHURCH SIGN NEAR YOU ...

YOU CAN'T WALK WITH GOD
AND HOLD HANDS WITH SATAN
AT THE SAME TIME.

FORBIDDEN FRUITS
CREATE MANY JAMS.

IT WASN'T THE APPLE,
IT WAS THE PAIR.

Living Courageously

The Lord is the One who will go before you.
He will be with you; He will not leave you or forsake you.
Do not be afraid or discouraged.

Deuteronomy 31:8 HCSB

Christian women have every reason to live courageously. After all, the final battle has already been won on the cross at Calvary. But even dedicated followers of Christ may find their courage tested by the inevitable disappointments and fears that visit the lives of believers and non-believers alike.

When you find yourself worried about the challenges of today or the uncertainties of tomorrow, you must ask yourself whether or not you are ready to place your concerns and your life in God's all-powerful, all-knowing, all-loving hands. If the answer to that question is yes—as it should be—then you can draw courage today from the source of strength that never fails: your Heavenly Father.

When once we are assured that God is good, then there can be nothing left to fear.

Hannah Whitall Smith

If a person fears God, he or she has no reason to fear anything else. On the other hand, if a person does not fear God, then fear becomes a way of life.

Beth Moore

What is courage? It is the ability to be strong in trust, in conviction, in obedience. To be courageous is to step out in faith—to trust and obey, no matter what.

Kay Arthur

SMILE!

A preacher visited an elderly woman from his congregation. As he sat on the couch, he noticed a large bowl of peanuts on the coffee table. "Mind if I have a few?" he asked. "No, not at all!" the woman replied.

They chatted for an hour and as the preacher stood to leave, he noticed he had eaten most of the bowl.

The preacher apologized, "I'm terribly sorry for eating all your peanuts; I really just meant to eat a few."

"Oh, that's all right," the woman said. "Ever since I lost my teeth all I can do is suck the chocolate off 'em."

Running on Empty

I will give you a new heart and put a new spirit in you . . . .

Ezekiel 36:26 NIV

For an extremely busy woman living in an extremely busy world, life may seem like a merry-go-round that never stops turning. If that description fits you, then you may find yourself running short of patience or strength, or both. If you're feeling exhausted or discouraged, there is a source from which you can draw the power needed to recharge your spiritual batteries. That source is God.

Have you "tapped in" to the power of God? Have you turned your life and your heart over to Him, or are you muddling along under your own power? The answer to these questions will determine the quality of your life here on earth and the destiny of your life throughout all eternity.

Are you tired or troubled? Turn your heart toward God in prayer. Are you weak or worried? Take the time—or, more accurately, make the time—to study God's Word. Do you feel like your emotional resources are almost gone? Call upon fellow believers to support you, and call upon Christ to renew your spirit and your life. When you do, you'll discover that the Creator of the universe can make everything new, including you.

REAL INSIGHTS

He is the God of wholeness and restoration.

Stormie Omartian

But while relaxation is one thing, refreshment is another. We need to drink frequently and at length from God's fresh springs, to spend time in the Scripture, time in fellowship with Him, time worshiping Him.

Ruth Bell Graham

If you're willing to repair your life, God is willing to help. If you're not willing to repair your life, God is willing to wait.

Marie T. Freeman

SMILE!

A passenger jet was suffering through a severe thunderstorm.

As the passengers were being bounced around by the turbulence, a young woman turned to a minister sitting next to her and, with a nervous laugh, asked, "Reverend, you're a man of God, can't you do something about this storm?"

To which he replied, "Lady, I'm in sales, not management."

The Wisdom to Be Generous

Freely you have received, freely give.

Matthew 10:8 NIV

God's gifts are beyond description, His blessings beyond comprehension. God has been incredibly generous with us, and He rightfully expects us to be generous with others. That's why the thread of generosity is woven into the very fabric of God's teachings.

In the Old Testament, we are told that, "The good person is generous and lends lavishly . . . ." (Psalm 112:5 MSG). And in the New Testament we are instructed, "Freely you have received, freely give" (Matthew 10:8 NKJV). These principles still apply. As we establish priorities for our days and our lives, we are advised to give freely of our time, our possessions, and our love—just as God has given freely to us.

Of course, we can never fully repay God for His gifts, but we can share them with others. And we should.

REAL INSIGHTS

The measure of a life, after all, is not its duration but its donation.

Corrie ten Boom

We can't do everything, but can we do anything more valuable than invest ourselves in another?

Elisabeth Elliot

Nothing is really ours until we share it.

C. S. Lewis

SMILE!

The preacher stepped up to the pulpit and cleared his throat. Then, he announced, "I have good news and bad news. The good news is we have enough money to retire the mortgage on the church."

A sigh of relief went through the congregation. The preacher continued: "The bad news is that most of that money is still in your pocket."

Radical Faith

I've laid down a pattern for you. What I've done, you do.

John 13:15 MSG

When it comes to your faith, are you "radical" or "run-of-the-mill"? Is your life radically different because of your relationship with Jesus, or are you the same person you were before you invited Him into your life?

Jesus wants to have a radical, life-altering relationship with you. Are you willing to have a radical relationship with Him? Unless you can answer this question with a resounding "Yes," you will rob yourself of the abundance that can and should be yours through Christ.

Ruth Bell Graham observed, "God's work is not in buildings, but in transformed lives." Are you a transformed person because of your relationship with the One from Galilee? Hopefully so. When you invited Christ to reign over your heart, you became a radically new creation. This day offers yet another opportunity to behave yourself like that new person. When you do, God will guide your steps and bless your endeavors . . . forever.

REAL INSIGHTS

Jesus challenges you and me to keep our focus daily on the cross of His will if we want to be His disciples.

Anne Graham Lotz

The Christian faith is meant to be lived moment by moment. It isn't some broad, general outline—it's a long walk with a real Person. Details count: passing thoughts, small sacrifices, a few encouraging words, little acts of kindness, brief victories over nagging sins.

Joni Eareckson Tada

It's your heart that Jesus longs for: your will to be made His own with self on the cross forever, and Jesus alone on the throne.

Ruth Bell Graham

COMING SOON TO A CHURCH SIGN NEAR YOU ...

A CHILD OF THE KING SHOULD BEAR
A FAMILY RESEMBLANCE.

WWJD = WALKING WITH JESUS DAILY.

I HAVE A FRIEND IN HIGH PLACES.

God's Good News

Thanks be to God for his indescribable gift!

2 Corinthians 9:15 NIV

Here's the great news: God's grace is not earned . . . and thank goodness it's not! If God's grace were some sort of reward for good behavior, none of us could earn enough brownie points to win the big prize. But it doesn't work that way. Grace is a free offer from God. By accepting that offer, we transform our lives today and forever.

God's grace is not just any old gift; it's the ultimate gift, and we owe Him our eternal gratitude. Our Heavenly Father is waiting patiently for each of us to accept His Son and receive His grace. Let us accept that gift today so that we might enjoy God's presence now and throughout all eternity.

In your greatest weakness, turn to your greatest strength, Jesus, and hear Him say, "My grace is sufficient for you, for My strength is made perfect in weakness" (2 Corinthians 12:9, NKJV).

Lisa Whelchel

SMILE!

A woman died and went to heaven where, of course, St. Peter met her at the pearly gates. St. Peter said, "Here's how it works. You need 100 points to make it into heaven. You tell me all the good things you've done, and I'll give you points based on each item, depending on how good it was. When you reach 100 points, you're in."

"Okay," the woman said, "I was married to the same man for 50 years and never cheated on him, not even in my heart."

"That's wonderful," said St. Peter, "That's worth three points!"

"Three points?" the woman said, feeling a little bit uncomfortable. "Well, that's not all. I attended church all my life and supported its ministry with my tithe and my service."

"Terrific!" said St. Peter. "That's certainly worth a point."

"Only one point?" the woman stammered. "Golly. How about this: I started a soup kitchen in my city and worked in a shelter for homeless veterans."

"Fantastic! That's good for two more points," St. Peter announced.

"ONLY TWO POINTS?!?" the woman cried. "At this rate the only way I will get into heaven is by the grace of God!"

Upon hearing these words, St. Peter smiled and said, "Come on in."

Excuses Everywhere

Each of us will be rewarded for his own hard work.

1 Corinthians 3:8 TLB

Excuses are everywhere . . . excellence is not. Whether you're a regular Jane or a corporate CEO, your work is a picture book of your priorities. So whatever your job description, it's up to you, and no one else, to become masterful at your craft. It's up to you to do your job right, and to do it right now.

Because we humans are such creative excuse-makers, all of the best excuses have already been taken—we've heard them all before.

So if you're wasting your time trying to concoct a new and improved excuse, don't bother. It's impossible. A far better strategy is this: do the work. Now. Then, let your excellent work speak loudly and convincingly for itself.

Making up a string of excuses is usually harder than doing the work.

Marie T. Freeman

REAL INSIGHTS

An excuse is only the skin of a reason stuffed with a lie.

Vance Havner

Replace your excuses with fresh determination.

Charles Swindoll

Our church was saddened to learn of the death of one of our most valued members: Someone Else. Someone's passing has created a vacancy that will be difficult to fill. Else has been with us for many years, and through thick and thin, Someone always did far more than a normal person's share of the work. Whenever there was a job to do, a class to teach, or a meeting to attend, one name was on everyone's list: "Let Someone Else do it." And whenever we needed leadership, Someone Else's named was always mentioned.

It was common knowledge that Someone Else was among the most liberal givers at our church. Whenever there was a financial need, everyone assumed Someone Else would make up the difference. Someone Else was a wonderful person; sometimes appearing superhuman, but in truth, we all expected too much of Someone Else. And now Someone Else is gone!

Someone Else has left us with a wonderful example to follow, but who is going to follow it? Who is going to do the things Someone Else did? The answer seems clear: since we can't depend on Someone Else, we must do the work ourselves.

Not in Denial

We justify our actions by appearances;
God examines our motives.

If we deny our sins, we allow those sins to flourish. And if we allow sinful behaviors to become habits, we invite hardships into our own lives and into the lives of our loved ones. When we yield to the distractions and temptations of this troubled world, we suffer. But God has other intentions, and His plans for our lives do not include sin or denial.

When we allow ourselves to encounter God's presence, He will lead us away from temptation, away from confusion, and away from the self-deception. God is the champion of truth and the enemy of denial. May we see ourselves through His eyes and conduct ourselves accordingly.

The single most important element in any human relationship is honesty—with oneself, with God, and with others.

Catherine Marshall

What I like about experience is that it is such an honest thing. You may take any number of wrong turnings; but keep your eyes open and you will not be allowed to go very far before the warning signs appear. You may have deceived yourself, but experience is not trying to deceive you. The universe rings true wherever you fairly test it.

C. S. Lewis

A college freshman began his first day of classes. His professor, who was clearly an atheist, started the class by saying, "Students, is there anyone here who can see God? If so, raise your hand. If there is anyone here who can hear God, raise your hand. If there is anyone who can smell God, raise your hand." After a short pause, with no response from the students, the professor concluded, "Since no one can see, smell, or hear God, there is no God."

The student then raised his hand, stood up, and addressed the class: "Can anybody here see the professor's brain? Can anyone hear the professor's brain? Can anyone smell the professor's brain?" After a short pause, the student concluded, "Since no one can see, hear, or smell the professor's brain, I conclude that he has no brain!"

The Ultimate Protection

The Lord is my rock, my fortress, and my deliverer, my God, my mountain where I seek refuge. My shield, the horn of my salvation, my stronghold, my refuge, and my Savior.

2 Samuel 22:2-3 HCSB

God has promised to protect us, and He intends to keep His promise. In a world filled with dangers and temptations, God is the ultimate armor. In a world filled with misleading messages, God's Word is the ultimate truth. In a world filled with more frustrations than we can count, God's Son offers the ultimate peace.

Will you accept God's peace and wear God's armor against the dangers of our world? Hopefully so—because when you do, you can live courageously, knowing that you possess the ultimate protection: God's unfailing love for you.

He goes before us, follows behind us, and hems us safe inside the realm of His protection.

Beth Moore

Prayer is our pathway not only to divine protection, but also to a personal, intimate relationship with God.

Shirley Dobson

The Will of God will never take you where the Grace of God will not protect you.

Anonymous

COMING SOON TO A CHURCH SIGN NEAR YOU ...

THE TASK AHEAD OF US
IS NEVER AS GREAT
AS THE POWER BEHIND US.

JESUS IS MY ROCK
'N I'M ON HIS ROLL.

The Right Kind of Fear

REAL LIFE DEVOTIONS AND FUNNY STORIES FOR WOMEN

The fear of the Lord is the beginning of knowledge,
but fools despise wisdom and discipline.

Proverbs 1:7 NIV

Are you a woman who possesses a healthy, fearful respect for God's power? Hopefully so. After all, God's Word teaches that the fear of the Lord is the beginning of knowledge (Proverbs 1:7).

When we fear the Creator—and when we honor Him by obeying His commandments—we receive God's approval and His blessings. But, when we ignore Him or disobey His commandments, we invite disastrous consequences.

God's hand shapes the universe, and it shapes our lives. God maintains absolute sovereignty over His creation, and His power is beyond comprehension. The fear of the Lord is, indeed, the beginning of knowledge. But thankfully, once we possess a healthy, reverent fear of God, we need never be fearful of anything else.

REAL INSIGHTS

When true believers are awed by the greatness of God and by the privilege of becoming His children, then they become sincerely motivated, effective evangelists.

Bill Hybels

The fear of God is the death of every other fear.

C. H. Spurgeon

The remarkable thing about fearing God is that when you fear God, you fear nothing else, whereas if you do not fear God, you fear everything else.

Oswald Chambers

SMILE!

A man fell off a cliff and was hanging precariously from a single tree branch. He cried out, "God, please help me!"

God answered, "Have faith, my son, and I will protect you. Just let go of that branch."

The man thought about it for a moment and then cried out again, "Is there anybody else up there?"

Who Will You Follow?

*If anyone would come after me,
he must deny himself and take up his cross and follow me.*

Mark 8:34 NIV

There's really no way around it: If you want to know God, you've got to get to know His Son. And that's good, because getting to know Jesus can—and should—be the most enriching experience of your life.

Can you honestly say that you're passionate about your faith and that you're really following Jesus? Hopefully so. But if you're preoccupied with other things—or if you're strictly a one-day-a-week Christian—then you're in need of a major-league spiritual makeover.

Jesus doesn't want you to be a lukewarm believer; Jesus wants you to be a "new creation" through Him. And that's exactly what you should want for yourself, too. Nothing is more important than your wholehearted commitment to your Creator and to His only begotten Son. Your faith must never be an afterthought; it must be your ultimate priority, your ultimate possession, and your ultimate passion.

You are the recipient of Christ's love. Accept it enthusiastically and share it passionately. Jesus deserves your undivided attention. And when you give it to Him, you'll be forever grateful that you did.

REAL INSIGHTS

I can tell you, from personal experience of walking with God for over fifty years, that He is the Lover of my soul.

Vonette Bright

It's your heart that Jesus longs for: your will to be made His own with self on the cross forever, and Jesus alone on the throne.

Ruth Bell Graham

A Sunday school teacher decided to have her young class memorize one of the most quoted passages in the Bible: Psalm 23. She gave the youngsters a month to learn the passage. Little Johnny was excited about the task, but, he just couldn't remember his lines. After much practice, he could barely get past the first verse.

On the day that the kids were scheduled to recite Psalm 23 in front of the congregation, Johnny was very nervous. When it was his turn, he stepped up to the microphone and said proudly, "The Lord is my Shepherd, and that's all I need to know."

Encouraging Others

*Let's see how inventive we can be in encouraging love
and helping out, not avoiding worshipping together
as some do but spurring each other on.*

Hebrews 10:24-25 MSG

One of the reasons that God placed you here on earth is so that you might become a beacon of encouragement to the world. As a faithful follower of the One from Galilee, you have every reason to be hopeful, and you have every reason to share your hopes with others. When you do, you will discover that hope, like other human emotions, is contagious.

As a follower of Christ, you are instructed to choose your words carefully so as to build others up through wholesome, honest encouragement (Ephesians 4:29). So look for the good in others and celebrate the good that you find. As the old saying goes, "When someone does something good, applaud—you'll make two people happy."

Encouraging others means helping people, looking for the best in them, and trying to bring out their positive qualities.

John Maxwell

REAL INSIGHTS

Words. Do you fully understand their power? Can any of us really grasp the mighty force behind the things we say? Do we stop and think before we speak, considering the potency of the words we utter?

Joni Eareckson Tada

As you're rushing through life, take time to stop a moment, look into people's eyes, say something kind, and try to make them laugh!

Barbara Johnson

COMING SOON TO A CHURCH SIGN NEAR YOU ...

A HUG IS THE IDEAL GIFT . . .
ONE SIZE FITS ALL.

SERVICE IS LOVE IN OVERALLS!

EXERCISE DAILY—
WALK WITH THE LORD!

God's Promises

*Patient endurance is what you need now,
so you will continue to do God's will.
Then you will receive all that he has promised.*

Hebrews 10:36 NLT

What do you expect from the day ahead? Are you willing to trust God completely, or are you living beneath a cloud of doubt and fear? God's Word makes it clear: you should trust Him and His promises, and when you do, you can live courageously.

For thoughtful Christians, every day begins and ends with God's Son and God's promises. When we accept Christ into our hearts, God promises us the opportunity for earthly peace and spiritual abundance. But more importantly, God promises us the priceless gift of eternal life.

Sometimes, especially when we find ourselves caught in the inevitable entanglements of life, we fail to trust God completely.

Are you tired? Discouraged? Fearful? Be comforted and trust the promises that God has made to you. Are you worried or anxious? Be confident in God's power. Do you see a difficult future ahead? Be courageous and call upon God. He will protect you and then use you according to His purposes. Are you confused? Listen to the quiet voice of your Heavenly Father. He is not a God of confusion. Talk with Him; listen to Him; trust Him, and trust His promises. He is steadfast, and He is your Protector . . . forever.

REAL INSIGHTS

We have ample evidence that the Lord is able to guide. The promises cover every imaginable situation. All we need to do is to take the hand he stretches out.

Elisabeth Elliot

Claim all of God's promises in the Bible. Your sins, your worries, your life—you may cast them all on Him.

Corrie ten Boom

Shake the dust from your past, and move forward in His promises.

Kay Arthur

SMILE!

One Sunday after church, a mom asked her very young son what the lesson was about. The boy answered, "Don't be scared, you'll get your quilt." Needless to say, the mom was perplexed.

Later in the day, the pastor stopped by for tea and the mom asked him what that morning's Sunday school lesson was about. He said, "Be not afraid, thy comforter is coming."

Too Many Distractions?

Let us lay aside every weight and the sin that so easily ensnares
us, and run with endurance the race that lies before us,
keeping our eyes on Jesus, the source and perfecter of our faith.

Hebrews 12:1-2 HCSB

All of us must live through those days when the traffic jams, the computer crashes, and the dog makes a main course out of our shoes. But, when we find ourselves distracted by the minor frustrations of life, we must catch ourselves, take a deep breath, and lift our thoughts upward.

Although we must sometimes struggle mightily to rise above the distractions of the everyday living, we need never struggle alone. God is here—eternal and faithful, with infinite patience and love—and, if we reach out to Him, He will restore our sense of perspective and give peace to our hearts.

Today, as an exercise in character-building, make this promise to yourself and keep it: promise to focus your thoughts on things that are really important, things like your faith, your family, your friends, and your future. Don't allow the day's interruptions to derail your most important work. And don't allow other people (or, for that matter, the media) to decide what's important to you and your family.

Distractions are everywhere, but, thankfully, so is God . . . and that fact has everything to do with how you prioritize your day and your life.

SMILE!

A pastor was giving a lesson to a group of children on the 23rd Psalm. He noticed that one of the little boys seemed disquieted by the phrase "Surely, goodness and mercy will follow me all the days of my life . . ."

"What's wrong with that, Johnny?" the pastor asked. "Well," answered Johnny, "I understand about having goodness and mercy, because God is good. But I'm not sure I want Shirley following me around all the time."

Too Impulsive?

Enthusiasm without knowledge is not good.
If you act too quickly, you might make a mistake.

Proverbs 19:2 NCV

Are you, at times, just a little bit impulsive? Do you occasionally leap before you look? Do you react first and think about your reaction second? If so, God wants to have a little chat with you.

God's Word is clear: as believers, we are called to lead lives of discipline, diligence, moderation, and maturity. But the world often tempts us to behave otherwise. Everywhere we turn, or so it seems, we are faced with powerful temptations to behave in undisciplined, ungodly ways.

God's Word instructs us to be disciplined in our thoughts and our actions; God's Word warns us against the dangers of impulsive behavior. God's Word teaches us that "anger" is only one letter away from "danger." And, as believers in a just God who means what He says, we should act—and react—accordingly.

REAL INSIGHTS

Waiting on God brings us to the journey's end quicker than our feet.

Mrs. Charles E. Cowman

The deepest spiritual lessons are not learned by His letting us have our way in the end, but by His making us wait, bearing with us in love and patience until we are able honestly to pray what He taught His disciples to pray: Thy will be done.

Elisabeth Elliot

God never hurries. There are no deadlines against which He must work. To know this is to quiet our spirits and relax our nerves.

A. W. Tozer

COMING SOON TO A CHURCH SIGN NEAR YOU ...

IF YOU DON'T AVOID THE BAIT ...
YOU'LL END UP ON THE HOOK.

A COLD CHURCH IS LIKE COLD BUTTER,
IT DOESN'T SPREAD WELL.

God's Abundance

I came that they may have life,
and have it abundantly.

John 10:10 NASB

Are you the kind of woman who accepts God's spiritual abundance without reservation? If so, you are availing yourself of the peace and the joy that He has promised. Do you sincerely seek the riches that our Savior offers to those who give themselves to Him? Then follow Him. When you do, you will receive the love and the abundance that Jesus offers to those who follow Him.

Seek first the salvation that is available through a personal, passionate relationship with Christ, and then claim the joy, the peace, and the spiritual abundance that the Shepherd offers His sheep.

If we were given all we wanted here, our hearts would settle for this world rather than the next.

Elisabeth Elliot

REAL INSIGHTS

Jesus intended for us to be overwhelmed by the blessings of regular days. He said it was the reason he had come: "I am come that they might have life, and that they might have it more abundantly."

Gloria Gaither

God is the giver, and we are the receivers. And His richest gifts are bestowed not upon those who do the greatest things, but upon those who accept His abundance and His grace.

Hannah Whitall Smith

SMILE!

A man and his wife were having an argument about who should brew the coffee. The husband said, "You are in charge of the cooking around here, so you should do it." The wife replied, "No, you should be the one to make the coffee because that's what it says in the Bible." The husband replied, "No way!" So she went to the bookshelf, opened up the New Testament, and stuck it under her husband's nose. Sure enough, there it was in black and white: "HEBREWS."

The Search for Purpose

The lines of purpose in your lives never grow slack, tightly tied as they are to your future in heaven, kept taut by hope.

Colossians 1:5 MSG

"What on earth does God intend for me to do with my life?" It's an easy question to ask but, for many of us, a difficult question to answer. Why? Because God's purposes aren't always clear to us. Sometimes we wander aimlessly in a wilderness of our own making. And sometimes, we struggle mightily against God in an unsuccessful attempt to find success and happiness through our own means, not His.

If you're a woman who sincerely seeks God's guidance, He will give it. But, He will make His revelations known to you in a way and in a time of His choosing, not yours, so be patient. If you prayerfully petition God and work diligently to discern His intentions, He will, in time, lead you to a place of joyful abundance and eternal peace.

Sometimes, God's intentions will be clear to you; other times, God's plan will seem uncertain at best. But even on those difficult days when you are unsure which way to turn, you must never lose sight of these overriding facts: God created you for a reason; He has important work for you to do; and He's waiting patiently for you to do it.

We set our eyes on the finish line, forgetting the past, and straining toward the mark of spiritual maturity and fruitfulness.

Vonette Bright

Each one of us is God's special work of art. Through us, He teaches and inspires, delights and encourages, informs and uplifts all those who view our lives. God, the master artist, is most concerned about expressing Himself—His thoughts and His intentions—through what He paints in our character . . . . [He] wants to paint a beautiful portrait of His Son in and through your life. A painting like no other in all of time.

Joni Eareckson Tada

COMING SOON TO A CHURCH SIGN NEAR YOU ...

EVERYONE YOU MEET TODAY
IS ON HEAVEN'S MOST WANTED LIST.

BE YE FISHERS OF MEN.
YOU CATCH THEM—
HE WILL CLEAN THEM.

A Willingness to Serve

Whoever wants to become great among you must serve the rest of you like a servant.

Matthew 20:26 NCV

Martha and Mary both loved Jesus, but they showed their love in different ways. Mary sat at the Master's feet, taking in every word. Martha, meanwhile, busied herself with preparations for the meal to come. When Martha asked Jesus if He was concerned about Mary's failure to help, Jesus replied, "Mary has chosen better" (Luke 10:42 NIV). The implication is clear: as believers, we must spend time with Jesus before we spend time for him. But, once we have placed Christ where He belongs—at the center of our hearts—we must go about the business of serving the One who has saved us.

How can we serve Christ? By sharing His message and by serving those in need. As followers of Jesus, we must make ourselves humble servants to our families, to our neighbors, and to the world. We must help the helpless, love the unloved, protect the vulnerable, and care for the infirm. When we do, our lives will be blessed by the One who sacrificed His life for us.

REAL INSIGHTS

God wants us to serve Him with a willing spirit, one that would choose no other way.

Beth Moore

So many times we say that we can't serve God because we aren't whatever is needed. We're not talented enough or smart enough or whatever. But if you are in covenant with Jesus Christ, He is responsible for covering your weaknesses, for being your strength. He will give you His abilities for your disabilities!

Kay Arthur

Christianity, in its purest form, is nothing more than seeing Jesus. Christian service, in its purest form, is nothing more than imitating him who we see. To see his Majesty and to imitate him: that is the sum of Christianity.

Max Lucado

A young girl observed plaques on the wall of the church building and asked her mother: "Mommy, why are those people's names on the wall?" The mother replied, "They are people who died in the service." Without blinking, the little girl asked, "Did they die in the morning or the evening service?"

Critics Beware

*Don't speak evil against each other, my dear brothers
and sisters. If you criticize each other and condemn each other,
then you are criticizing and condemning God's law.
But you are not a judge who can decide whether the law
is right or wrong. Your job is to obey it.*

James 4:11 NLT

From experience, we know that it is easier to criticize than to correct. And we know that it is easier to find faults than solutions. Yet the urge to criticize others remains a powerful temptation for most of us. Our task, as obedient believers, is to break the twin habits of negative thinking and critical speech.

Negativity is highly contagious: we give it to others who, in turn, give it back to us. This cycle can be broken by positive thoughts, heartfelt prayers, and encouraging words. As thoughtful servants of a loving God, we can use the transforming power of Christ's love to break the chains of negativity. And we should.

Judging draws the judgment of others.

Catherine Marshall

REAL INSIGHTS

Being critical of others, including God, is one way we try to avoid facing and judging our own sins.

Warren Wiersbe

I still believe we ought to talk about Jesus. The old country doctor of my boyhood days always began his examination by saying, "Let me see your tongue." That's a good way to check a Christian: the tongue test. Let's hear what he is talking about.

Vance Havner

SMILE!

A Sunday school teacher was asking her students some questions after a series of lessons on God's omnipotence. She asked, "Is there anything God can't do?" All the children were silent.

Finally, one boy held up his hand. The teacher, on seeing this, was disappointed that the child had missed the point of the lesson.

She sighed and asked, "Well, what is it you think God can't do?" The boy replied, "He can't please everybody."

Big Dreams

Live full lives, full in the fullness of God. God can do anything, you know—far more than you could ever imagine or guess or request in your wildest dreams!
He does it not by pushing us around but by working within us, his Spirit deeply and gently within us.

Ephesians 3:19-20 MSG

Are you willing to entertain the possibility that God has big plans in store for you? Hopefully so. Yet sometimes, especially if you've recently experienced a life-altering disappointment, you may find it difficult to envision a brighter future for yourself and your family. If so, it's time to reconsider your own capabilities . . . and God's.

Your heavenly Father created you with unique gifts and untapped talents; your job is to tap them. When you do, you'll begin to feel an increasing sense of confidence in yourself and in your future.

It takes courage to dream big dreams. You will discover that courage when you do three things: accept the past, trust God to handle the future, and make the most of the time He has given you today.

Nothing is too difficult for God, and no dreams are too big for Him—not even yours. So start living—and dreaming—accordingly.

The future lies all before us. Shall it only be a slight advance upon what we usually do? Ought it not to be a bound, a leap forward to altitudes of endeavor and success undreamed of before?

Annie Armstrong

You cannot out-dream God.

John Eldredge

The visiting preacher was really getting the congregation moving. Near the end of his sermon he said, "This church has really got to walk!"—to which someone in the back yelled, "Let her walk, preacher!"

The preacher then raised his voice: "If this church is going to get going, it's got to get up and run!" —to which someone again yelled with gusto, "Let her run, preacher!"

Feeling the surge of the church, the preacher then shouted, "If this church is going to go, it's got to really fly," and once again, with great gusto, someone yelled, "Let her fly, preacher; let her fly!"

The preacher then seized the moment and screamed, "If this church is really going to fly, it's going to need money!" —to which someone in the back yelled, "Let her walk, preacher; let her walk."

Your Testimony

*And I say to you, anyone who acknowledges Me before men,
the Son of Man will also acknowledge him before
the angels of God; but whoever denies Me before men
will be denied before the angels of God.*

Luke 12:8-9 HCSB

L et's face facts: those of us who are Christians should be willing to talk about the things that Christ has done for us. Our personal testimonies are vitally important, but sometimes, because of shyness or insecurities, we're afraid to share our experiences. And that's unfortunate.

In his second letter to Timothy, Paul shares a message to believers of every generation when he writes, "God has not given us a spirit of timidity" (1:7). Paul's meaning is crystal clear: When sharing our testimonies, we must be courageous and unashamed.

We live in a world that desperately needs the healing message of Christ Jesus. Every believer, each in his or her own way, bears responsibility for sharing the Good News of our Savior. And it is important to remember that we bear testimony through both words and actions.

If you seek to be a radical follower of Christ, then it's time for you to share your testimony with others. So today, preach the Gospel through your words and your deeds . . . but not necessarily in that order.

There is nothing anybody else can do that can stop God from using us. We can turn everything into a testimony.

Corrie ten Boom

Faith in small things has repercussions that ripple all the way out. In a huge, dark room a little match can light up the place.

Joni Eareckson Tada

Claim the joy that is yours. Pray. And know that your joy is used by God to reach others.

Kay Arthur

COMING SOON TO A CHURCH SIGN NEAR YOU . . .

IT'S GOOD TO BE SAVED
AND KNOW IT!
IT'S ALSO GOOD TO BE SAVED
AND SHOW IT!

WHEN YOU DON'T WITNESS,
YOU JUST DID.

Today's Decisions

The righteous one will live by his faith.

Habakkuk 2:4 HCSB

Everyday life is an adventure in decision-making. Each day, we make countless decisions that hopefully bring us closer to God. When we live according to God's commandments, we share in His abundance and His peace. But, when we turn our backs upon God by disobeying Him, we bring needless suffering upon ourselves and upon our families.

Do you seek God's peace and His blessings? Then obey Him. When you're faced with a difficult choice or a powerful temptation, seek God's counsel and trust the counsel He gives. Invite God into your heart and live according to His commandments. When you do, you will be blessed today and tomorrow and forever.

REAL INSIGHT

When we do what is right, we have contentment, peace, and happiness.

Beverly LaHaye

Holiness is not an impossibility for any of us.

Elisabeth Elliot

Righteousness comes only from God.

Kay Arthur

SMILE!

A minister told his congregation, "Next week I plan to preach about the sin of lying. To help you understand my sermon, I want you all to read Mark 17."

The following Sunday, as he prepared to deliver his sermon, the minister asked for a show of hands. He wanted to know how many had read Mark 17.

Every hand went up. The minister smiled and said, "Mark has only 16 chapters. I will now proceed with my sermon on the sin of lying."

Your Wonderful Life

I have set before you life and death, blessings and curses.
Now choose life, so that you and your children may live
and that you may love the LORD your God,
listen to his voice, and hold fast to him.

Deuteronomy 30:19-20 NIV

Life can be tough sometimes, but it's also wonderful—and it's a glorious gift from God. How will you use that gift? Will you treat this day as a precious treasure from your Heavenly Father, or will you take the next 24 hours for granted? The answer should be obvious: Every day, including this one, comes gift-wrapped from God—your job is to unwrap that gift, to use it wisely, and to give thanks to the Giver.

Instead of sleepwalking through life, you must wake up and live in the precious present. Each waking moment holds the potential to celebrate, to serve, to share, or to love. Because you are a person with incalculable potential, each moment has incalculable value. Your challenge is to experience each day to the fullest as you seek to live in accordance with God's plan for your life. When you do, you'll experience His abundance and His peace.

Are you willing to treat this day (and every one hereafter) as a special gift to be savored and celebrated? You should—and if you seek to Live with a capital L, you most certainly will.

REAL INSIGHTS

The Christian life is motivated, not by a list of do's and don'ts, but by the gracious outpouring of God's love and blessing.

Anne Graham Lotz

Life is simply hard. That's all there is to it. Thank goodness, the intensity of difficulty rises and falls. Some seasons are far more bearable than others, but none is without challenge.

Beth Moore

Life is a glorious opportunity.

Billy Graham

COMING SOON TO A CHURCH SIGN NEAR YOU ...

IN THIS LIFE IT'S NOT WHAT YOU HAVE
BUT WHO YOU HAVE THAT COUNTS!

IF YOU'RE READY TO DIE—
YOU'RE READY TO LIVE!

LIVE LIFE SO THAT THE PREACHER
WON'T HAVE TO LIE AT THE FUNERAL.

His Eternal Love

For the Lord is good, and His love is eternal;
His faithfulness endures through all generations.

Psalm 100:5 HCSB

God is love. It's a sweeping statement, a profoundly important description of what God is and how God works. God's love is perfect. When we open our hearts to His perfect love, we are touched by the Creator's hand, and we are transformed.

Barbara Johnson observed, "We cannot protect ourselves from trouble, but we can dance through the puddles of life with a rainbow smile, twirling the only umbrella we need—the umbrella of God's love."

As the English mystical writer Juliana of Norwich noted, "We are so preciously loved by God that we cannot even comprehend it. No created being can ever know how much and how sweetly and tenderly God loves them."

So today, even if you can only carve out a few quiet moments, offer sincere prayers of thanksgiving to your Father. Thank Him for His blessings and His love.

The greatest honor you can give Almighty God is to live gladly and joyfully because of the knowledge of His love.

Juliana of Norwich

REAL INSIGHT

Jesus loves us with fidelity, purity, constancy, and passion, no matter how imperfect we are.

Stormie Omartian

After forty years of shaving himself every morning, a man in a small Southern town decided he had enough. He told his wife that he intended to let the local barber shave him from now on. He went to the shop, which was owned by the pastor of their Baptist church. The barber's wife, Grace, was working that day so she performed the task.

Grace shaved him, sprayed him with lilac water, and said, "That will be $20." The man thought it a bit high, but paid the bill and went to work.

The next morning he looked in the mirror and his face was just as smooth as it had been when he left the barbershop the day before. "Not bad," he thought. "At least I don't need to get a shave every day." The next morning the man's face was still smooth.

Two weeks later, no whiskers had grown back. It was more than the man could take, so he returned to the barbershop. "I thought $20 was high for a shave," he told the barber's wife, "but you must have done a great job. It's been two weeks and my whiskers still haven't started growing back."

"Of course they haven't," the barber's wife replied. "You have been shaved by Grace. Once shaved, always shaved."